THE JOINERS

A Sociological Description of

Voluntary Association Membership

in the United States

by

MURRAY HAUSKNECHT

The Bedminster Press
New York
1962

Copyright © 1962, The Bedminster Press, New York

Printed in the United States of America

Library of Congress Catalogue Card No. 61-15579

THE JOINERS

ACKNOWLEDGEMENTS

At all stages of the research and writing of this study I have had the benefit of the comments and criticisms of Professor Hans L. Zetterberg, and his contribution is reflected in whatever merits the work may possess. I have also profited from critical readings of a draft of this manuscript by Professors Theodore Abel, Conrad Arensberg, Daniel Bell, Herbert Hyman, and David Truman. Conversations with Richard Maisel on problems of analysis of survey research data were of considerable help in facilitating my work.

I am indebted to both Professor Charles R. Wright and Professor Hyman for permitting me to use material on which they had first call. I am similarly indebted to Dr. David Sills of the Bureau of Applied Social Research. But for their generosity this study could not have been undertaken. My thanks are also due to the National Opinion Research Center for allowing me to use the data of one of their surveys, and, in particular, to Mr. Paul B. Sheatsley for his invaluable assistance.

This work could not have been begun or carried through to completion without the understanding, patience, and encouragement of my wife.

TABLE OF CONTENTS

CHAPTER I

INTRODUCTION

When Alexis de Tocqueville observed that in the United States "there is no end which human will despairs of attaining through the combined power of individuals united in a society"[1] a stereotype was born—the American as a joiner. It is a stereotype enriched by a cluster of caricatures representing variations on the theme: the benevolent and protective Elk; the hearty Rotarian; the genealogy-proud Daughter of the American Revolution; the arid, humorless temperance union crusader; etc. The persistence of the theme and variations is almost in itself sufficient reason for undertaking, as a matter of pure anthropological curiosity, an investigation of voluntary association membership to see whether or not there is still any reality to the notion of the American as a joiner. But the number of association members and their location within the society are questions intimately related to profound social problems, and so any research of the extent of membership is ultimately concerned with something more than what appears to be a cultural idiosyncracy.

Social theory has traditionally linked the voluntary association with the problems of the maintenance of a stable political democracy. Thus, De Tocqueville distinguished between the association in Europe and America; "one a weapon . . . an army" to be used in direct and extra-legal conflict for power, the other a legal means for countering the "moral power of the majority" and persuading others to a specific opinion.[2] This definition of the role and functions of the voluntary association remains an important focus for theory and research. A contemporary American sociologist, Arnold Rose, in proposing "a theory of the functions of voluntary associations in the contemporary social structure," stated that they "play a major role in American democracy." He goes on to specify three major functions: voluntary associations prevent a concentration and centralization of power; they help individuals in understanding how political processes operate; and they are mechanisms for social change.[3]

---

1. *Democracy in America* (New York: Vintage Books, 1954), Vol. 1, p. 199.
2. *Ibid.*, p. 203.
3. Arnold Rose, *Theory and Method in the Social Sciences* (Minneapolis: University of Minnesota Press, 1954), pp. 50f.

These, of course, are summary statements; following through from this perspective an even more specific list of politically relevant functions of associations may be derived.

By uniting in a voluntary association, those with common interests strengthen themselves in the struggle for the enhancement and protection of those interests. Association members are more easily made aware of their interests, and they formulate appropriate opinions with respect to specific problems they face. Once these opinions have been crystallized the association facilitates the spread of the opinion so as to influence others. The association, then, is a means for involving the individual in the social and political processes of the society. Hence, as an association member the individual has another source of exposure to and contact with what is occurring in the larger society. The association, therefore, may be said to have consequences of an educational nature. It provides factual knowledge of events; tends to promote insight into and understanding of the significance of events; and a knowledge of, as it were, the mechanics of government and society generally. Since the association is part of the political and social processes of the society it may also help train future social leaders and serve as a channel for their emergence into the society.

In addition to these functions of more or less direct political relevance, social theory stresses functions of associations linked to other problems of a contemporary society, yet still connected to the problem of maintaining a stable democratic political and social structure. These are important functions in terms of a given perspective:

> Prior to the Industrial Revolution, the community, the church, and the extended family were able, in large measure, to satisfy whatever felt needs there were for human fellowship, personal security, and "explanation" of the forces controlling the perceived world. The Industrial Revolution was the strongest of a series of major social changes that drastically weakened the all-encompassing community, church, and extended family. These changes exerted their influence through a rise in geographic mobility, urbanization, and secularization . . .[4]

Here the emphasis is upon the functions of associations for the psychological needs of individuals as social persons. The association brings those isolated from human ties—a result of living in industrial and urban communities—back into interaction with other human beings. More generally, the association allows individuals to transcend their immediate life situations and serves to integrate them with the broader

---

4. *Ibid.,* p. 103.

community and society. The satisfaction of psychological needs by associations has political relevance; if these needs are met by association membership, "the voluntary association would tend to contribute to the democratic character of American society, since strong family systems, churches, and communities tend to be totalitarian in their influence over the individual, whereas voluntary associations distribute and diversify power and influence."[5] To this may be added the point made by theorists of mass society: individuals isolated from others and poorly integrated into the society are more susceptible to the influence of anti-democratic ideologies.[6]

Social theory, then, assigns to voluntary associations a critical role in contemporary democratic societies. But do associations, in fact, perform these functions? More specifically, do voluntary associations in America in the middle of the twentieth century actually function toward the ends assigned to them by social theory? Answers to questions like these must rest on empirical grounds. That is, before one can discuss the theoretical issues involved or accept the implicit picture of the functioning of democratic processes resulting from the acceptance of the theory, it is necessary to have valid and reliable data about the extent of membership in voluntary associations; data about the characteristics of those who join and who do not join; data about the types of associations they are affiliated with, etc.

It was with these empirical problems in mind that the present research was undertaken: a description of the extent of voluntary association membership in the United States based upon the statistics of two surveys, one in 1954 and the other in 1955, of national samples of the population.

To say that the study is descriptive means that it has been designed to provide empirical data of the type referred to above. This, of course, does not imply that statements, hypotheses, or speculations of an explanatory or interpretative nature are avoided; it does mean that this more analytical orientation is subordinated to a more purely descriptive one.

Previous reports on voluntary association membership have with one exception, been based upon partial samples of the population.[7] The

---

5. *Ibid.*, p. 59.
6. See for example, William Kornhauser, *The Politics of Mass Society* (Glencoe, Ill.: The Free Press, 1960), pp. 102ff.
7. The exception is: Charles R. Wright and Herbert Hyman, "Voluntary Association Membership of American Adults: Evidence from National Sample Surveys," *American Sociological Review*, 23 (June, 1958), 284-294. For further information about the samples used here see Appendix A.

statistics on membership have been gathered either in the course of traditional sociological community studies or by surveys of urban area populations. Since these previous researches report on a segment of the total society their value is impaired by the uncertainty about how far their results may be generalized for the society as a whole. Thus, methodological considerations aside, it may fairly be asked, for example, whether what is true of membership in a town or city of New England will also be true of a similar community in another part of the country. A point of major significance about the present study is that it is based upon statistics drawn from samples of the entire population—any finding may validly be stated as a generalization applying to the society as a whole.

Technically speaking, the data to be presented are the results of a "secondary analysis," i.e., the data were gathered in the course of survey researches directed toward other problems than those which occupy us here. Any secondary analysis is limited to raising questions which can be answered by the available data, therefore relevant questions often cannot be raised, much less answered. In the present instance, however, this is not a significant handicap. The standardization of some survey research procedures very often results in the "automatic" collection of data adequate for most descriptive purposes. The two surveys used here provide between them almost all the relevant information for our needs, although there are some unavoidable gaps. On the other hand, because there is a considerable overlap in the data provided by each of them, there is in most instances a "built-in" check on the reliability of the reported findings.

Previous research on the problem has indicated a strong correlation between socio-economic status and membership as well as a correlation between membership and urbanization. In the second chapter we examine the evidence from national samples on the relationship between these variables and voluntary association membership. Following that, in Chapter III, the statistics pertaining to the relationship between membership and other variables, described loosely as "life cycle" variables, are presented. Chapter IV reports the findings on the relationship between membership and other characteristics and identifications of individuals, e.g., religious preference.

In these three chapters there is no attempt made to distinguish among different kinds of voluntary associations; they are treated as a gross category. However, in Chapter V we shift to a description of membership in terms of *types* of associations; that is, our concern is with the kinds of associations different segments of the society join.

As we have pointed out above, our concern with description does not rule out attention to more analytical questions, and in Chapter VI this becomes the central orientation. The primary interest there is with data drawn from the surveys which test certain hypotheses about the functions of voluntary association membership for attitudes and behavior.

The concluding chapter is an assessment of the significance of the findings in terms of the role and functions of voluntary association.

CHAPTER II

STRATIFICATION AND URBANIZATION

All previous studies of membership in voluntary associations in the United States show that social stratification and size of community are important determinants of membership rates. Therefore, in the following pages we are interested in whether or not the statistics based upon national cross-section samples will confirm the role of these variables in determining voluntary association membership.

How Many Belong?

First, however, we shall examine the over-all picture. Table 2:1 shows the percentage of Americans who belong and do not belong to voluntary associations.[1] Since almost all previous surveys on voluntary association of Americans have shown that the membership rate is low rather than high, the most interesting aspect of the results here is the lack of agreement between the two samples. Only 36 per cent, just a bit over a third, of the NORC sample belong to associations while 55 per cent of those questioned by AIPO belong.

As a more detailed discussion in Appendix A points out, the difference between these two percentages is related to differences between the two surveys. While neither of the surveys is concerned with problems of voluntary association membership, the AIPO survey was explicitly interested in the individual's knowledge of certain kinds of organizations, e.g., the Red Cross, the National Foundation for Infantile Paralysis, etc., and whether or not he had contributed to their fund raising campaigns or had participated in those campaigns. The latent function of this line of questioning was to direct the respondent's attention to voluntary associations and his relationship to them, and so most of the questions preceding the one about membership served to stimulate recall of his own affiliations. In addition, claims of voluntary association membership where none existed may have functioned as an unconscious or conscious defense in a situation in which a negative answer to questions about contributions and participation could easily

---

1. In each chapter the tables follow the text.

be perceived as damaging to self-esteem.[2] None of these factors is present in the NORC survey. The question about association membership came at the tail end of a long and complex interview, and it had no discernible relationship to what had gone before. Thus, while the AIPO figure may be somewhat inflated as a result of an interview schedule encouraging "distortion," the reported NORC percentage may not accurately reflect reality because of respondent and interviewer fatigue. In addition, definitions of voluntary association membership varied between the two surveys. The AIPO survey figures for membership include memberships in trade unions, while the NORC survey did not count union membership as voluntary association membership. Finally, the phrase "in the community here" occurring in the NORC survey's question may have biased the results.

The survey figures, then, should be defined as representing a range, and therefore the proper way of reading Table 2:1 is: "Between 55 per cent and 36 per cent of all adult Americans belong to voluntary associations." But the disagreement in magnitude between the samples does not have, *per se,* any bearing on statements about relationships between membership and any given variable. If we find, for example, that middle class rates of membership are higher than working class rates of membership in both samples but that the AIPO percentages for each class are higher than the NORC percentages for the same class, this difference in magnitude does not effect the conclusion that the direction of results in two samples is strong corroboration for the statement that there is an important relationship between membership and class position.

To return to Table 2:1: it is interesting to note that despite the proliferation of voluntary associations catering to practically every conceivable specialized interest, no more than 25 per cent of the population belongs to more than one association.

A High Educational Level . . .

However, the members of associations are not distributed uniformly

---

2. The influence of this factor on responses has been empirically investigated. In one study respondents were asked whether they had registered at the polls and voted, contributed to a Community Chest drive, possessed a library card, *etc.*, and the replies of each respondent were checked against official records. The level of validity, i.e., the extent to which the responses conformed to the observed facts, was very low when a negative answer meant violation of strong social expectations. As an example particularly pertinent to the present discussion, fully *one-third* of the respondents reported they had contributed to the Community Chest but in reality had *not* contributed. Hugh J. Parry and Helen M. Crossley, "Validity of Responses to Survey Questions," *Public Opinion Quarterly,* 14 (Spring, 1950), 61-80.

throughout the society. This is very apparent when we stratify the respondents according to indices of socio-economic status. Tables 2:2A
and 2:2B, for example, show that as the educational level increases
membership in voluntary associations increases. The difference between
the extremes in each sample is striking. In Table 2:2A 39 per cent of
the least educated are members of associations, while among college
graduates over 78 per cent are affiliated with associations. Similarly,
the NORC survey found 17 per cent of the least educated to be
members but 61 per cent of the college educated to be members.

And a High Income . . .

If education makes a difference, Tables 2:3A and 2:3B indicate that
income also makes a difference: as income increases so does the rate of
membership. Once more the extremes in each sample illustrate the
point. In Table 2:3A, 46 per cent of the lowest income group are
members while this is true for 69 per cent whose incomes are over $7000
a year. Of those in the lowest income group in the NORC sample only
24 per cent are members as contrasted with 52 per cent of the highest
income group who are members.

Plus a White Collar Job . . .

When we classify individuals by occupation, from data provided
only by the NORC survey, Table 2:4 summarizes the conclusions
drawn from the other indices of socio-economic status. In occupational
categories characteristic of the upper range of the middle class—professional, managerial, etc.—53 per cent of the respondents are members, but among those in clerical and sales occupations 41 per cent are
members. Not only is the membership rate of individuals in working
class occupations lower than that of those holding higher status jobs,
there is a difference in rates between the upper working class and those in
the lower reaches. Among skilled workers 32 per cent are joiners while
among those in the service occupations and unskilled jobs 27 per cent
and 21 per cent, respectively, join associations.

The results are unambiguous: No matter what index of social stratification is used, the higher the class position the greater the rate of voluntary association membership.

The Metropolis and the Small Town

When we turn to the variable of size of community and its relationship to membership, each of the samples must be discussed separately,

because each utilizes different categories. Looking first, then, at Table 2:5A we note that as the size of the *urban* community decreases the rate of membership increases from 47 per cent for communities with populations of over 250,000 to 68 per cent for communities between 2500 and 9000 people. An urban community with a population between these two extremes also has an intermediate membership rate, e.g., 60 per cent of the respondents living in cities with populations between 10 and 50 thousand belong to associations. Among those living in non-urban areas between 56 per cent and 58 per cent are joiners. The highest rates of membership, then, tend to be found in the smaller urban communities.

In a general way the findings reported in Table 2:5B confirm these results. Of those living in the most populous metropolitan areas 32 per cent are members, and of those living in less populated metropolitan areas 36 per cent are affiliated with associations. In the more urbanized counties 39 per cent of the sample were members, but this is not significantly different from the membership rate found in less urbanized counties where 38 per cent of the population joins at least one association. We may conclude that there is a relationship between population density and membership in voluntary associations, just as there is a relationship between class and membership. An obvious question: Does the latter relationship persist at each level of urbanization?

Before we answer the question we should note an interesting paradox. The most fertile ground for the proliferation of voluntary associations is large urban communities, but we find the largest percentage of members in smaller ones. There are at least three possible reasons for this. One involves the problem of the available opportunities for leisure time "investments." A metropolis offers many opportunities for the pursuit of leisure time interests which do not entail association membership. These same interests may exist in smaller communities, but there are fewer resources for satisfying them. Thus, the voluntary associations of the metropolis must compete with the museum, the concert hall, the theater, etc. Second, the sheer number of people in a metropolis makes it easier to satisfy needs which in a small community can be satisfied only within the framework of an association. So, for example, a college educated woman who had embarked on a career before she married is more likely to find others similar to herself in her neighborhood if she lives in a large city; there are more like her because the city is a magnet for them. In a small community the chapter of the American Association of University Women or the League of Women Voters may be the only means by which such women can seek one another out and maintain contact. Finally, voluntary associations may induce in the individual living in a small town a greater sense of "potency"; a sense that, as it were, "his vote counts." Some associations may be important for the community as a whole, and in a small town it is easier to get a feeling that this is so. The resident of megalopolis is apt to feel that both he and his association are ultimately impotent—"you can't fight City Hall"—and this is hardly an orientation which encourages joining an association. On the other hand, if this latter attitude does exist, it may be part of a cyclical process in which the feeling of impotence is itself a result of a low rate of membership.

Income and Size of Community

When we examine the relationship between income and community size, Table 2:6A, we see that in each category of community size membership increases as income increases. In cities of more than 50,000 people 37 per cent of the lowest income group—incomes of less than $3000 a year—are members, while in the highest income category—annual income of $5000 or more—59 per cent belong to associations. In smaller urban communities, those with populations between 2,500 and 50,000, 58 per cent of the lowest income group belong and 68 per cent of the highest are members. The same pattern holds in the non-urban communities. In rural non-farm communities and farm areas the lowest income groups have membership rates of 51 per cent and 48 per cent, respectively, as compared with 67 per cent and 79 per cent of the individuals with the highest incomes living in the respective types of communities.

This pattern is duplicated in the findings of the NORC survey reported in Table 2:6B. At the lowest income level there is no significant difference in membership rates between the two types of metropolitan areas—22 per cent in the larger and 21 percent in the smaller ones—but this membership rate increases among those earning $5,000 a year or more, since 32 per cent of this group in larger metropolitan areas belong and 47 per cent in the smaller metropolitan areas are members. Similarly in the more urbanized counties, 25 per cent of the lowest income group are members and 28 per cent belong in the least urbanized counties, while among those with highest incomes in these two types of areas 63 per cent and 47 per cent respectively are joiners.

In addition, the results of both surveys indicate a general pattern of a rise in membership rate for each income level as the size of community decreases. There are two exceptions: Table 2:6A shows that the lowest income groups in rural areas have lower rates than in small cities, and in Table 2:6B we find that the rate of membership of the highest income group in the least urbanized counties decreases. Rates of membership, then, increase with income regardless of community size, and each income group tends to increase its rate of membership as the level of urbanization declines.

Education and Size of Community

A pattern similar to the one just described appears when the relationship between education and membership within each type of community is examined. In Table 2:7A when we compare those with only an elementary school education and the college educated who live in the large cities we see that 38 per cent of the former group belong while 58 per cent of the latter join associations. In the smaller cities 55 per cent of the least educated are members, and 22.5 per cent of those who attended college belong. The picture is the same in rural areas: 41 per cent of those with the least education in rural non-farm communities belong as over against 86 per cent with most education, and in farm areas the membership rates at these two educational levels are 50 per cent and 88 per cent respectively.

Turning now to our other survey, Table 2:7B shows that in both large and small metropolitan areas approximately one-fifth of those with an elementary school education join associations while 49 per cent of the college educated in the large metropolitan areas and 59 per cent of this group in the smaller metropolitan areas belong. When the more urbanized and less urbanized counties are compared we see that 22 per cent and 27 per cent, respectively, of the least educated are members of associations, while 72.5 per cent of the college educated are joiners in the more urbanized counties and 52 per cent of this group join in the less urbanized counties.

Occupation and Size of Community

We may note, without reporting the results in detailed form, that the data obtained by the NORC survey on the relationship between occupation and membership in various communities conforms to the patterns found above. So, for example, in the largest metropolitan areas, among professionals and managers and proprietors 33 per cent and 49 per cent respectively are members of associations; in the same communities 27 per cent of the skilled workers and 23 per cent of the semi-skilled and unskilled workers belong. In the least urbanized counties 58 per cent of the professionals and 51 per cent of the managers and proprietors join associations. Among the skilled and semi-skilled in these areas 40 per cent and 27 per cent respectively are members of associations.

Taking income, education, and occupation as indices of social stratification we may summarize our findings in this context by saying size of community and urbanization effects all classes in the same fashion. That is, while the initial class differences in rates of voluntary association membership hold for all communities regardless of size, there is a general trend for membership rates for *each* class to increase as the size of community increases.

Previous Research

In 1952 the Survey Research Center at the University of Michigan asked a subsample of 542 respondents about membership in voluntary associations as part of their election survey of that year. Despite the fact that the size of the sample is too small to be highly reliable, it is a *national* sample and as such is directly comparable with the two samples used in the present study. Interestingly enough, the over-all results of the SRC research is at odds with the findings of both the AIPO and NORC surveys: 64 per cent of the SRC sample belong to at least one voluntary association. However, once we set aside questions relating to magnitude we find that the SRC results run in the same direction as the results described above with respect to stratification. Thus, on the same indices of socio-economic status—income, education, and occupation—there is a strong relationship with membership. The categories of community types make comparisons with the AIPO and the NORC survey results difficult, but the lower rate for rural areas as compared with urban communities is generally congruent with the results reported here. (Lane, 1960, p. 78)[3]

As we noted at the outset, the relationship between class and membership has been a consistent feature of all previous studies of voluntary association membership regardless of composition of the sample. So, for example, both Komarovsky's 1946 report on the New York metropolitan area and Axelrod's 1956 report on the Detroit metropolitan area show that middle class individuals have higher rates of membership than working class individuals. (Komarovsky, 1946; Axelrod, 1956) At the other extreme, Hay, reporting on four rural communities in the Northeast, also finds the same relationship as does Brown's research on three rural communities in Pennsylvania. (Hay, 1950; Brown, 1953)

---

3. References here are to the Bibliography.

Zimmer and Hawley ignore the rural-urban dichotomy and compare a central city with its fringe area, but the relationship between class and membership still holds in both areas. This same research also found, however, a higher rate of membership over-all in the city than in the fringe. (Zimmer and Hawley, 1959b) A somewhat similar research was conducted by Foskett who compared two Oregon communities located in the same general geographical area: a rapidly growing community and one with a stable population level. Participation rates were similar in both communities, and the usual relationship between class and participation obtained. (Foskett, 1955)

Finally, we may note some information about voluntary association membership in other countries. Zetterberg reports that 51 per cent of a national sample of Swedes belong to at least one association exclusive of membership in churches, unions, cooperatives, and if membership in these associations were to be included then "virtually every adult Swede belongs to an association." (Zetterberg, 1960.) The relationship between class and membership was found in the Swedish survey, and a survey using a national sample finds this to be true of Norway as well. (Rokkan, 1959) A survey of a large Finnish industrial city found that the better educated are more apt to be members and to participate more in associations than the less well educated. (Allardt and Pesonen, 1960) In France a survey of a national sample shows that 41 per cent of all adults belong to at least one association. (Rose, 1954) In Guadelajara, Mexico's second largest city, Dotson found that the over-all level of membership in associations was small, but that the class and membership were related in the usual fashion. (Dotson, 1953) Mayntz cites a German study which shows that "there is no clear trend in the rates of membership when communities of different sizes are compared, from small rural to large metropolitan." (Reigrotzki, 1956, cited in Mayntz, 1960) Banfield's research on a Southern Italian farm community reveals no relationship between class and membership; on the other hand, no voluntary associations of any kind existed in the town. (Banfield, 1958)

Table 2:1

MEMBERSHIP IN VOLUNTARY ASSOCIATIONS: TWO NATIONAL SAMPLES OF AMERICANS, 1954 AND 1955

Per Cent Belonging to	*AIPO**	*NORC***
None	45%	64%
One	30	20
Two	16	9
Three plus	9	7
Total Belonging	55%	36%
Total	(2000) 100%	(2379) 100%

*"What organizations or clubs, like church organizations, service clubs, fraternal clubs, do you belong to?" (1954)
**"Do you happen to belong to any groups or organizations in the community here?" (1955)

Table 2:2A

MEMBERSHIP IN VOLUNTARY ASSOCIATIONS: BY EDUCATION — AIPO SAMPLE

	Per Cent Who Belong to				
Education	*None*	*One*	*Two or More*	*Total*	
Some Elementary School	61%	28%	11%	100%	(286)
Elementary School Graduate	52	33	15	100	(447)
Some High School	47	30	23	100	(438)
High School Graduate	36	32	32	100	(528)
Some College	30	29	41	100	(159)
College Graduate	22	23	55	100	(126)

Table 2:2B

MEMBERSHIP IN VOLUNTARY ASSOCIATIONS: BY EDUCATION — NORC SAMPLE

		Per Cent Who Belong to		
			Two or	
Education	*None*	*One*	*More*	*Total*
Some Elementary School	83%	12%	5%	100% (348)
Elementary School Graduate	73	17	10	100 (522)
Some High School	67	20	13	100 (495)
High School Graduate	57	23	20	100 (610)
Some College	46	24	30	100 (232)
College Graduate	39	25	36	100 (170)

Table 2:3A

MEMBERSHIP IN VOLUNTARY ASSOCIATIONS: BY INCOME — AIPO SAMPLE

		Per Cent Who Belong to		
			Two or	
Income	*None*	*One*	*More*	*Total*
Under $2000	54%	31%	15%	100% (507)
$2000-$2999	47	31	22	100 (362)
$3000-$3999	42	29	29	100 (398)
$4000-$4999	40	33	27	100 (317)
$5000-$6999	37	26	37	100 (254)
$7000+	31	30	39	100 (102)

Table 2:3B

MEMBERSHIP IN VOLUNTARY ASSOCIATIONS: BY INCOME — NORC SAMPLE

Income	None	One	Per Cent Who Belong to Two or More	Total	
Under $2000	76%	17%	7%	100%	(385)
$2000-$2999	71	17	12	100	(304)
$3000-$3999	71	18	11	100	(379)
$4000-$4999	65	21	14	100	(450)
$5000-$7499	57	22	21	100	(524)
$7500+	48	22	30	100	(328)

Table 2:4

MEMBERSHIP IN VOLUNTARY ASSOCIATIONS: BY OCCUPATION — NORC SAMPLE

Occupation	None	One	Per Cent Who Belong to Two or More	Total	
Professional	47%	24%	29%	100%	(259)
Proprietors, Managers, Officials	47	24	29	100	(294)
Farm Owners	58	28	14	100	(265)
Clerical and Sales	59	21	20	100	(240)
Skilled Labor	68	19	13	100	(447)
Semi-Skilled Labor	77	14	9	100	(492)
Service	73	18	9	100	(142)
Non-Farm Labor	79	16	5	100	(155)
Farm Labor	87	13	0	100	(54)
Retired, Unemployed	77	11	12	100	(35)

Table 2:5A

MEMBERSHIP IN VOLUNTARY ASSOCIATIONS: BY SIZE OF COMMUNITY — AIPO SAMPLE

| Per Cent Belonging to | *In Thousands* | | | | | |
	over 250	*50-249*	*10-49*	*2.5-9*	*Rural non-Farm*	*Farm*
None	53%	47%	40%	32%	44%	42%
One	27	33	33	34	26	34
Two plus	20	20	27	34	30	24
Total	100	100	100	100	100	100
	(461)	(245)	(274)	(194)	(520)	(306)

Table 2:5B

MEMBERSHIP IN VOLUNTARY ASSOCIATIONS: BY SIZE OF COMMUNITY — NORC SAMPLE

Per Cent Belonging to	Metropolitan Area Over One Million	Metropolitan Area Less Than One Million	County Largest Town 10-50,000	County No Town as Large as 10,000
None	68%	64%	61%	62%
One	18	19	19	23
Two plus	14	17	20	15
Total	100	100	100	100
	(731)	(653)	(460)	(470)

Table 2:6A

MEMBERSHIP IN VOLUNTARY ASSOCIATIONS: BY SIZE OF COMMUNITY AND INCOME — AIPO SAMPLE

Per Cent Belonging to	*50,000 and Over*			*2,500-49,999*		
	Under $3,000	*$3,000-$4,999*	*$5,000 or More*	*Under $3,000*	*$3,000-$4,999*	*$5,000 or More*
None	63%	48%	41%	42%	35%	32%
One	26	33	27	35	32.5	29
Two plus	11	19	32	23	32.5	39
Total	100	100	100	100	100	100
	(213)	(316)	(161)	(198)	(160)	(92)

	Rural Non-Farm			*Farm*		
	Under $3,000	*$3,000-$4,999*	*$5,000 or More*	*Under $3,000*	*$3,000-$4,999*	*$5,000 or More*
None	49%	40%	33%	42%	25%	21%
One	28	23	26	34	37	27
Two plus	23	37	41	14	38	52
Total	100	100	100	100	100	100
	(260)	(174)	(70)	(198)	(65)	(33)

The Joiners

Table 2:6B

MEMBERSHIP IN VOLUNTARY ASSOCIATIONS: BY SIZE OF COMMUNITY AND INCOME — NORC SAMPLE

Per Cent Belonging to	Metropolitan Area Over One Million			Metropolitan Area Less Than One Million		
	Under $3,000	*$3,000- $4,999*	*$5,000 or More*	*Under $3,000*	*$3,000- $4,999*	*$5,000 or More*
None	78%	74%	58%	79%	69%	53%
One	14	16	20	15	18	23
Two plus	8	10	12	6	13	24
Total	100	100	100	100	100	100
	(114)	(280)	(329)	(160)	(201)	(286)

	County Largest Town 10-50,000			County No Town as Large as 10,000		
	Under $3,000	*$3,000- $4,999*	*$5,000 or More*	*Under $3,000*	*$3,000- $4,999*	*$5,000 or More*
None	75%	67%	37%	72%	56%	53%
One	12	19	27	18	27	24
Two plus	13	14	36	10	17	23
Total	100	100	100	100	100	100
	(158)	(175)	(126)	(208)	(164)	(96)

Table 2:7A

MEMBERSHIP IN VOLUNTARY ASSOCIATIONS: BY SIZE
OF COMMUNITY AND EDUCATION — AIPO SAMPLE

Per Cent Belonging to	50,000 or More			2,500-49,999		
	Elementary School	High School	College	Elementary School	High School	College
None	62%	50%	32%	45%	36%	22.5
One	24	31	29	38	34	22.5
Two plus	14	19	39	17	30	55
Total	100	100	100	100	100	100
	(216)	(375)	(123)	(157)	(221)	(84)

	Rural Non-Farm			Farm		
	Elementary School	High School	College	Elementary School	High School	College
None	59%	34%	24%	50%	38%	12%
One	25	29	30	42	28	31
Two plus	16	37	56	8	34	57
Total	100	100	100	100	100	100
	(219)	(234)	(62)	(141)	(136)	(26)

Table 2:7B

MEMBERSHIP IN VOLUNTARY ASSOCIATIONS: BY SIZE OF COMMUNITY AND EDUCATION — NORC SAMPLE

Per Cent Belonging to	*Metropolitan Area Over One Million*			*Metropolitan Area Less Than One Million*		
	Elementary School	*High School*	*College*	*Elementary School*	*High School*	*College*
None	81%	66%	51%	82%	62%	41%
One	12	19	22	11	21	27
Two plus	7	15	27	7	17	32
Total	100	100	100	100	100	100
	(216)	(369)	(146)	(209)	(320)	(124)

	County Largest Town 10-50,000			*County No Town as Large as 10,000*		
	Elementary School	*High School*	*College*	*Elementary School*	*High School*	*College*
None	78%	58%	27.5%	73%	55%	48%
One	13	22	27.5	19	27	20
Two plus	9	20	45	8	18	32
Total	100	100	100	100	100	100
	(194)	(192)	(73)	(206)	(209)	(54)

CHAPTER III

SEX, AGE, AND MARRIAGE

While class and community size are clearly important determinants of voluntary association membership, it is equally obvious that membership will vary with other aspects of the life situations of individuals. Thus, we may hypothesize that membership rates will be determined by such things as sex and marriage roles as well as by religion, race, etc. In the present chapter we shall be concerned with the influence of some of these other variables; those which can be thought of as representing aspects of the life cycle of individuals. In view of the critical role of class and urbanization, we shall examine, whenever feasible in this and the following chapter, the extent to which relationships are conditioned by these variables.

Sex and Membership

As can be seen from Table 3:1, men and women join associations in equal numbers. Thus the AIPO survey found that 54 per cent of the men and 57 per cent of the women are members of associations while the NORC survey reports that 36 per cent of each sex belongs. This lack of difference between the sexes with respect to membership is uneffected by class factors. In Tables 3:2A and 3:2B, which report the relationship between income, sex, and membership, we see that the rate of membership for both men and women increases as the level of income increases. So, for example, about one-fourth of the men and women in the lowest income group of Table 3:2B are members whereas 46 per cent of the men and 49 per cent of women with family incomes of at least $5000 a year are voluntary association members. Similarly with education: In Tables 3:3A and 3:3B we find that the greater the level of educational attainment the greater the membership rate for both sexes. In Table 3:2A, for example, less than half of the men and women with an elementary school education are members, but about 75 per cent of both sexes who had a college education are affiliated with voluntary associations.

When we raise the question of possible differences in membership rates between men and women within each class the evidence is inconsistent. The AIPO survey results, Table 3:2A, show that 47 per cent of the men and 50 per cent of the women at the lowest income level are joiners, and in Table 3:2B we see that NORC results run in the same direction at this level—23 per cent of the men and 29 per cent of the women are members. But when the rates of membership are compared at the highest income level the results of the two surveys are contradictory. Table 3:2A shows that 68 per cent of the men and 63 per cent of the women are members of associations, while in Table 3:2B the percentages run in the opposite direction, i.e., 46 per cent of the men and 49 per cent of the women belong. The same lack of consistency is found when education is used as an index of class. So, for example, we see from Table 3:3A that 43 per cent of the men and 47 per cent of the women with the least years of schooling are members, but in Table 3:3B 23 per cent of both sexes join associations.

However, when we turn to the membership rates of men and women as related to the size of the community some differences between the sexes begin to appear. This is most apparent in the figures of Table 3:4A. In the largest cities 51 per cent of the males and 47 per cent of the females are members of associations, but in smaller urban communities 60 per cent of the males are members while 67 per cent of the females belong. This tendency for more women than men to join associations in smaller communities is also apparent in rural non-farm areas where 59 per cent of the women and 52 per cent of the men are joiners. A similar tendency is found in the statistics presented by Table 3:4B. In the metropolitan areas we find practically no difference in the rates of membership of men and women, but in the two less urbanized areas we find that 37 per cent and 35 per cent of the men are members while in both instances 40 per cent of the women join associations. These differences are probably related to the fact that there is a larger proportion of women who work in larger communities than in smaller ones.

Age and Membership

When age is treated as an independent variable we note in Tables 3:5A and 3:5B, despite differences in categorization, that the youngest and oldest age groups have the lowest rates, although the rates of the latter groups remain at a higher point than those of the younger groups. The pattern of the relationship of age and association membership can be seen in detail in Table 3:5B. In the youngest group in the sample, those between 21 and 25 years of age, only 16 per cent are members, but this rises sharply to 36 per cent for those in the 25 to 35 age group. The percentage of those who are members rises once again to 42 per cent in the next age group, those between 35 and 45. However, the percentage of members declines to 36 per cent for those between 45 and 55; remains at about the same level, 39 per cent, for the next age group; and declines still further to 32 per cent for those over 65. The same general pattern is apparent in the figures of Table 3:5A.

In other words, the distribution of members by age for both samples resembles a normal curve slightly skewed toward the upper age ranges. There is a steady rise in the number of members to a peak at about 40 years of age, and from then on there is a decline, but it is not as steep as the rise in membership from the age of 20 to 40 and does not return to the same low point. It would seem, then, that as one advances toward middle age there is a tendency to become a joiner, but as one grows older there is a tendency to shed one's memberships. On the other hand, we may speculate that the large percentage of members among the middle age groups may be due to their early experience with the Depression when circumstances tended to facilitate the joining of organizations.

If we ignore the middle groups, then from another perspective these figures are an illustration of the integration of the young American into his society as he assumes career and family responsibilities, and a gradual detachment from society as he approaches old age.

We have already seen that there is no relationship between sex and membership in voluntary associations. But when we treat sex and age as joint variables this initial finding does not continue to hold.

Table 3:6A shows that when age is controlled men under 40 have a higher rate of membership than women, but after age 40 women are members in greater numbers than men. Thus, 61 per cent of the men between the ages of 30 and 39 belong to associations and 57 per cent of the women at this age level are members, but of all those between 50 and 59 years of age 55 per cent of the men are members and 62 per cent of the women belong.

The results reported for the NORC sample, Table 3:6B, conform to the general pattern of the AIPO sample. Up to the age of 44 there is a general tendency for men to have a higher rate of membership than women, and in the oldest age group we note a reversal which shows women with a higher rate of membership.

Since we have already noted that the young have lower membership rates than the old, when we examine the effect of age upon membership with indices of socio-economic status (SES) held constant the respondents in each sample are divided into two age groups. In the AIPO sample the cutting point is at 40 years of age, and in the NORC sample the cutting point is at age 35.

In Tables 3:7A and 3:7B we see that membership rates increase for both age groups as income rises. At each income level, however, the older individuals consistently have higher rates of affiliation than younger individuals. The importance of income is indicated by the interesting fact that 43 per cent of the younger individuals earning $5,000 or more a year in the NORC sample (Table 3:7B) are members of associations, while only 28 per cent of the *older group* in the lowest income bracket are members; i.e., younger men with high incomes have higher rates than older men with lower incomes. Similarly in the AIPO sample: Of those between 20 and 40 years of age at the highest income level 60 per cent are members, while 51 per cent of those over 40 and earning less than $3000 a year are members.

This same general pattern emerges once more in Tables 3:8A and 3:8B, where education is the index of SES. Membership rates for both age groups increase with an increase in the level of educational attainment; membership rates are higher for the older people at each educational level; and the younger group at the highest educational level has a higher rate of membership than the older group at the elementary school level.

Tables 3:9A and 3:9B record the relationship between community size, age, and membership. Table 3:9A shows that the now familiar pattern that older individuals have a higher rate of membership in voluntary associations than younger ones may still be found in the largest urban communities. This finding is confirmed by the NORC survey results reported in Table 3:9B: those over 35 years of age have higher membership rates than those in their twenties and early thirties.

But Table 3:9A also shows that the difference between the age groups becomes less significant in the smaller communities. Indeed, a finer breakdown would show that in communities with populations of more than 2500 people but less than 10,000 persons 68 per cent of the younger age group and 67 per cent of the older age group are members of voluntary associations, i.e., in these communities there is no difference between the groups. The same lack of difference is apparent in Table 3:9A for the rural non-farm population. However, older individuals in the farm population have higher rates than do younger persons. The tendency for differences between the two groups to disappear with decreasing urbanization is confirmed by the figures in Table 3:9B. When we compare the two types of counties, less urbanized regions with the metropolitan areas, we note no appreciable differences in the former and significant differences between the age groups in the latter.

These results are of some interest in the light of our previous hypothesis that the over-all tendency for the rate of voluntary association membership to increase with age reflects the relative "lack of integration" of the young in the society. Our present findings indicate, at the very least, that the "integration of the young" is more problematic in the urban areas than in the less urban areas.

Marital Status and Membership

In discussing the relationship between age and membership we suggested that our results showed that as individuals assumed career and family responsibilities there was an increase in the rate of membership in voluntary associations. The most obvious finding of Tables 3:10A and 3:10B, which report the relationship between marital status and membership, tends to bear out this suggestion. In Table 3:10A, for example, 57 per cent of the married individuals belong to associations and 44 per cent of the single people are members. Similarly, among the widowed and those with broken marriages the membership rate is 53 per cent and 46 per cent respectively.

It was also suggested in our previous discussion that up to a certain point increasing age is symbolic of increasing integration into the society. This suggestion, too, receives some support when we compare the membership figures of the widowed and divorced with those of the single and married. In both samples the rate of membership for the former groups resembles the rate for the single rather than the married. For example, in Table 3:10B 30 per cent of the widowed and 27 per cent of the divorced and separated are members, while 38 per cent of the married belong to associations.

Previous Research

The Survey Research Center's national sample results are in conformity with the findings reported in this chapter for age and for sex. That is, the SRC survey shows no significant difference between the sexes, and again we see that the youngest and oldest groups in the population have the lowest membership rates while the middle groups tend to have the highest rates. (Lane, 1960, p. 78)

The surveys using national samples contradict earlier research results based upon more limited samples. For example: In Middletown a greater percentage of men belong to associations than women. (Lynd and Lynd, 1929, p. 528) Similarly, in Yankee City more men than women are members of associations, and the same holds true for Bennington. (Warner and Lunt, 1941; Scott, 1947) In Chicago, too, the membership rate of men exceeds that of women. (Goldhamer, 1942)

When we turn to the influence of class upon membership Komarovsky reports that only in the lower socio-economic groups, where more men than women belong, are there significant differences between the sexes. (Komarovsky, 1946) In Yankee City, however, women in the three highest strata have a higher rate than comparable men, and the reverse is true for the three lowest strata. (Warner and Lunt, 1941) In Dotson's small sample of the New Haven working class more men than women belong to associations. (Dotson, 1951)

Our findings with respect to age are generally congruent with other researches. Thus, in Bennington, while differences between age levels are not statistically significant, the number of memberships held increases with age, and the high point occurs at the 40-54 age level. (Scott, 1947) In Detroit, according to Axelrod, there is a relatively low rate in early adulthood, a high rate of membership for individuals about 40 years old, and a new low rate among those in their sixties. (Axelrod, 1954, cited in Bell and Force, 1956a) Similarly, in two North Carolina rural areas the same general pattern obtains. (Mayo, 1950) An interesting finding with respect to age is reported by Zimmer and Hawley: In Flint, Michigan, there is the usual difference between the younger individuals and old ones relative to membership, but in the city's fringe area there are no significant differences among the age groups. (Zimmer and Hawley, 1959b)

Table 3:1

MEMBERSHIP IN VOLUNTARY ASSOCIATIONS: BY SEX

Per Cent Belonging to	AIPO		NORC	
	Men	Women	Men	Women
None	46%	43%	64%	64%
One	29	31	21	19
Two plus	25	26	15	17
Total	100	100	100	100
	(986)	(988)	(1114)	(1255)

Table 3:2A

MEMBERSHIP IN VOLUNTARY ASSOCIATIONS: BY INCOME AND SEX — AIPO SAMPLE

Per Cent Belonging to	Under $3,000		$3,000-$4,000		$5,000 or More	
	Male	Female	Male	Female	Male	Female
None	53%	50%	43%	39%	32%	37%
One	31	30	27	25	30	25
Two plus	16	20	30	26	38	38
Total	100	100	100	100	100	100
	(425)	(437)	(358)	(346)	(178)	(170)

Table 3:2B

MEMBERSHIP IN VOLUNTARY ASSOCIATIONS: BY INCOME AND SEX — NORC SAMPLE

Per Cent Belonging to	Under $3,000		$3,000-$4,000		$5,000 or More	
	Male	*Female*	*Male*	*Female*	*Male*	*Female*
None	77%	71%	66%	69%	54%	51%
One	15	18	23	17	22	23
Two plus	8	11	11	14	24	26
Total	100	100	100	100	100	100
	(303)	(385)	(376)	(449)	(431)	(408)

Table 3:3A

MEMBERSHIP IN VOLUNTARY ASSOCIATIONS: BY EDUCATION AND SEX — AIPO SAMPLE

Per Cent Belonging to	Elementary School		High School		College	
	Male	*Female*	*Male*	*Female*	*Male*	*Female*
None	57%	53%	41%	41%	25%	29%
One	31	30	29	33	26	27
Two plus	12	17	30	26	49	44
Total	100	100	100	100	100	100
	(394)	(331)	(431)	(524)	(149)	(131)

Table 3:3B

MEMBERSHIP IN VOLUNTARY ASSOCIATIONS: BY EDUCATION AND SEX — NORC SAMPLE

Per Cent Belonging to	Elementary School		High School		College	
	Male	*Female*	*Male*	*Female*	*Male*	*Female*
None	77%	77%	62%	61%	43%	42%
One	16	14	22	22	27	23
Two plus	7	9	16	17	30	35
Total	100	100	100	100	100	100
	(438)	(429)	(467)	(634)	(208)	(191)

Table 3:4A

MEMBERSHIP IN VOLUNTARY ASSOCIATIONS: BY SIZE OF COMMUNITY AND SEX — AIPO SAMPLE

Per Cent Belonging to	50,000 or More		2,500- 49,000		Rural Non-Farm		Farm	
	Male	*Female*	*Male*	*Female*	*Male*	*Female*	*Male*	*Female*
None	49%	53%	40%	33%	48%	41%	44%	40%
One	28	30	33	34	21	30	37	32
Two plus	23	17	27	33	31	29	19	28
Total	100	100	100	100	100	100	100	100
	(343)	(357)	(227)	(234)	(254)	(257)	(162)	(140)

Table 3:4B

MEMBERSHIP IN VOLUNTARY ASSOCIATIONS: BY SIZE OF COMMUNITY AND SEX — NORC SAMPLE

Per Cent Belonging to	*Metropolitan Area Over One Million*		*Metropolitan Area Less Than One Million*		*County Largest Town 10-50,000*		*County No Town as Large as 10,000*	
	Male	*Female*	*Male*	*Female*	*Male*	*Female*	*Male*	*Female*
None	68%	67%	63%	66%	63%	60%	65%	60%
One	18	17	21	17	20	18	21	24
Two plus	14	16	16	17	17	22	14	16
Total	100	100	100	100	100	100	100	100
	(349)	(382)	(294)	(359)	(209)	(251)	(243)	(227)

Table 3:5A

MEMBERSHIP IN VOLUNTARY ASSOCIATIONS: BY AGE — AIPO SAMPLE

Per Cent Belonging to	20-29	30-39	40-49	50-59	60+
None	54%	41%	41%	42%	44%
One	28	29	34	29	31
Two plus	18	30	25	29	25
Total	100	100	100	100	100
	(398)	(498)	(409)	(300)	(372)

Table 3:5B

MEMBERSHIP IN VOLUNTARY ASSOCIATIONS: BY AGE — NORC SAMPLE

Per Cent Belonging to	*21-24*	*25-34*	*35-44*	*45-54*	*55-64*	*65+*
None	84%	64%	58%	64%	61%	68%
One	10	21	23	19	20	19
Two plus	6	15	19	17	19	13
Total	100	100	100	100	100	100
	(138)	(594)	(523)	(457)	(328)	(292)

Table 3:6A

MEMBERSHIP IN VOLUNTARY ASSOCIATIONS: BY AGE AND SEX — AIPO SAMPLE

	Per Cent Who Belong to				
Age and Sex	*None*	*One*	*Two or More*	**Total**	
20-29					
Men	53%	24%	23%	100%	(162)
Women	55	32	13	100	(231)
30-39					
Men	39	28	33	100	(241)
Women	43	30	27	100	(251)
40-49					
Men	44	34	22	100	(194)
Women	40	33	27	100	(210)
50-59					
Men	45	28	27	100	(176)
Women	38	30	32	100	(119)
60 and over					
Men	49	32	19	100	(204)
Women	39	29	32	100	(163)

Table 3:6B

MEMBERSHIP IN VOLUNTARY ASSOCIATIONS: BY AGE AND SEX — NORC SAMPLE

	Per Cent Who Belong to			
Age and Sex	*None*	*One*	*Two or More*	*Total*
21-24				
Men	77%	18%	5%	100% (56)
Women	89	5	6	100 (82)
25-34				
Men	65	23	12	100 (255)
Women	64	19	17	100 (328)
35-44				
Men	57	24	19	100 (251)
Women	59	22	19	100 (272)
45-54				
Men	64	18	18	100 (227)
Women	64	21	15	100 (230)
55-64				
Men	61	21	18	100 (178)
Women	61	17	22	100 (150)
65 and over				
Men	77	15	8	100 (129)
Women	62	22	16	100 (163)

Table 3:7A

MEMBERSHIP IN VOLUNTARY ASSOCIATIONS: BY INCOME AND AGE — AIPO SAMPLE

Per Cent Belonging to	*Under $3,000*		*$3,000-$4,999*		*$5,000 or More*	
	20-39	*40+*	*20-39*	*40+*	*20-39*	*40+*
None	55%	49%	43%	39%	40%	30%
One	29	31	31	30	23	31
Two plus	16	20	26	31	37	39
Total	100 (320)	100 (540)	100 (387)	100 (320)	100 (168)	100 (182)

Table 3:7B

MEMBERSHIP IN VOLUNTARY ASSOCIATIONS: BY INCOME AND AGE — NORC SAMPLE

Per Cent Belonging to	*Under $3,000*		*$3,000-$4,999*		*$5,000 or More*	
	21-34	*35+*	*21-34*	*35+*	*21-34*	*35+*
None	79%	72%	72%	65%	57%	51%
One	13	18	17	21	24	22
Two plus	8	10	11	14	19	27
Total	100	100	100	100	100	100
	(149)	(529)	(329)	(484)	(247)	(578)

Table 3:8A

MEMBERSHIP IN VOLUNTARY ASSOCIATIONS: BY EDUCATION AND AGE — AIPO SAMPLE

Per Cent Belonging to	*Elementary School*		*High School*		*College*	
	20-39	*40+*	*20-39*	*40+*	*20-39*	*40+*
None	64%	53%	45%	35%	33%	20%
One	26	32	30	32.5	26	26
Two plus	10	15	25	32.5	41	54
Total	100	100	100	100	100	100
	(181)	(544)	(560)	(393)	(147)	(136)

Table 3:8B

MEMBERSHIP IN VOLUNTARY ASSOCIATIONS: BY EDUCATION AND AGE — NORC SAMPLE

Per Cent Belonging to	Elementary School		High School		College	
	21-34	35+	21-34	35+	21-34	35+
None	88%	76%	69%	56%	50%	38%
One	8	16	19	24	26	24
Two plus	4	8	12	20	24	38
Total	100	100	100	100	100	100
	(119)	(736)	(462)	(620)	(151)	(242)

Table 3:9A

MEMBERSHIP IN VOLUNTARY ASSOCIATIONS: BY SIZE OF COMMUNITY AND AGE — AIPO SAMPLE

Per Cent Belonging to	50,000 or More		2,500-49,000		Rural Non-Farm		Farm	
	20-39	40+	20-39	40+	20-39	40+	20-39	40+
None	54%	49%	38%	35%	45%	44%	48%	37%
One	28	30	33	34	24	26	30	38
Two plus	18	21	29	31	31	30	22	13
Total	100	100	100	100	100	100	100	100
	(322)	(379)	(208)	(253)	(236)	(277)	(130)	(172)

Table 3:9B

MEMBERSHIP IN VOLUNTARY ASSOCIATIONS: BY SIZE OF COMMUNITY AND AGE — NORC SAMPLE

Per Cent Belonging to	*Metropolitan Area Over One Million*		*Metropolitan Area Less Than One Million*		*County Largest Town 10-50,000*		*County No Town as Large as 10,000*	
	21-34	*35+*	*21-34*	*35+*	*21-34*	*35+*	*21-34*	*35+*
None	72%	65%	71%	61%	64%	61%	61%	63%
One	16	18	16	21	23	17	21	23
Two plus	12	17	13	18	13	22	18	14
Total	100	100	100	100	100	100	100	100
	(243)	(477)	(197)	(440)	(149)	(306)	(136)	(329)

Table 3:10A

MEMBERSHIP IN VOLUNTARY ASSOCIATIONS: BY MARITAL STATUS — AIPO SAMPLE

Per Cent Belonging to	*Married*	*Single*	*Widowed*	*Divorced & Separated*
None	43%	56%	47%	54%
One	30	30	30	15
Two plus	27	14	23	31
Total	100	100	100	100
	(1618)	(150)	(180)	(46)

Table 3:10B

MEMBERSHIP IN VOLUNTARY ASSOCIATIONS: BY MARITAL STATUS — NORC SAMPLE

Per Cent Belonging to	Married	Single	Widowed	Divorced & Separated
None	62%	72%	70%	73%
One	21	14	20	17
Two plus	17	14	10	10
Total	100	100	100	100
	(1888)	(200)	(192)	(86)

CHAPTER IV

MEMBERSHIP AND INTEGRATION

In the last chapter it was suggested that the low rate of membership in voluntary associations among the young and the old was a reflection of the relative lack of integration of these groups with the larger society. This theme of the integration of individuals with the society is the common thread which will run through our examination of the relationship between membership and such variables as race, religion, and political party identification.

Owners and Renters

What is meant by "integration with the society" in this context is illustrated by contrasting home owners with those who rent their homes. The latter tend to be a more mobile group; they are less likely to remain in neighborhoods for the same length of time as home owners.[1] We may anticipate, therefore, that they are less likely to establish strong relationships with their neighbors and to join associations which have their roots in the local neighborhood. Moreover, the home owner by virtue of the major economic investment represented by his home, if for no other reason, is more apt to feel that he has a "stake in" both his neighborhood and the wider community. It is in this sense that home ownership may be understood as linking the individual with the society.

That there is some connection between the status of owner or renter and membership in voluntary associations may be seen in Table 4:1. While 43 per cent of the owners belong to at least one association only 25 per cent of those who rent their homes are members.

Since home ownership does represent an economic investment, it is possible that the correlation with a high rate of membership merely masks the effects of socio-economic status. However, as Tables 4:2 and 4:3 show, this is not a spurious relationship. When the highest and lowest income groups of Table 4:2 are compared we see that among owners earning less than $3000 a year 36 per cent are members as

---

1. Peter Rossi, *Why People Move* (Glencoe, Ill.: The Free Press, 1955), pp. 65ff. "Home ownership" and "rent" are, of course, crude indices of mobility. Unfortunately in neither of the samples is it possible to distinguish the mobile individuals more precisely. In addition, a bias may have been introduced by the wording of the question.

opposed to the 15 per cent of the renters with the same incomes who belong to associations, and while 51 per cent of the owners at highest income level belong only 37 per cent of the renters with similar incomes are members. In Table 4:3, among the owners with an elementary school education 29 per cent are members, while among renters at the same level of education 14 per cent join associations. Again, when the rates among the college educated are compared, 63 per cent of the owners belong to associations and 47 per cent of the renters are members. Clearly, the effect of home ownership is independent of the effects of income and education.

Implicit in our use of size of community as a variable is the proposition that, as population increases, the potential for situations is greater in which large numbers of heterogeneous individuals exist in relative isolation from one another and unable to establish strong social relationships. We have already seen, as one kind of evidence of the validity of this assumption, that as far as urban communities are concerned there is a lower rate of membership in the larger communities than in the smaller ones. However, if the interpretation of the significance of home ownership is correct, we should also expect that even in the most heavily populated communities there will be differences between owners and renters.

That such differences do appear may be seen in Table 4:4. We note, first, that home owners have a consistently higher rate of membership, regardless of how urbanized the region is. That is, in both metropolitan areas 42 per cent of the owners and 33 per cent of the renters belong to associations. Even in the two less urbanized areas owners tend to be members in greater numbers than renters. In these areas 49 per cent and 40 per cent of the owners belong, while among renters in these regions 25 per cent and 35 per cent are members. Secondly, if we compare the largest metropolitan area with the least urbanized county we see that membership rates for both owners and renters increase as the degree of urbanization decreases, but this is not a straight line increase.

That is, in *both* metropolitan areas the rates for the two groups are similar, and it is not until we reach the most urbanized county that we find a change in the rate—at that, significant only for the owners. The rate for renters rises significantly only in the least urbanized region.

When we turn to the relationship with age the effect of home ownership is marked. In Table 4:5 we see that among owners 41 per cent of the young and 44 per cent of the old are members, and among the renters 25 per cent of the younger individuals and 26 per cent of the older ones join associations. In other words, the previously noted differences between the age groups tend to disappear. This pattern is consistent with the hypothesis that the low rate of voluntary association membership of the younger persons was a reflection of the general "lack of integration" of the young into the society, and that the growth in membership rate with age is a reflection of the greater integration into the society that accompanies the assumption of adult roles in the family and occupational spheres.

The young home owner is not only one who is more likely to have already assumed fully fledged family and occupational roles but, in addition, is one for whom the mere fact of ownership of his own home is a tangible symbol of position and status within the community. His house serves to locate him, as it were, within the social system. Therefore, it follows that when we compare individuals who have fully assumed adult roles their membership rates will be similar despite their differences in age. Conversely, if one is less integrated into the society the rate of voluntary association membership should drop regardless of age. The lack of difference in the rates of young and old renters—mobile individuals who by definition tend to be less integrated by virtue of their mobility and who lack a significant symbol of "place" within the social system—is also consistent with the hypothesis.

In our previous discussion we also noted that in Tables 3:9A and 3:9B the differences between the age groups almost disappeared in rural areas. Why this occurs is now somewhat clearer: communities in the latter areas tend, on the whole, to be more traditional, homogeneous, and, of course, smaller. In such a community it is easier for the young to locate themselves. In larger communities, more heterogeneous and industrialized, it is more difficult for the young to perceive "where they fit into" the social system.[2]

Political Party Identification and Membership

Given the American party system, it may be difficult at first to perceive the common thread which connects the variable of identification with a political party with that of home ownership. But the connection is easily apparent in Table 4:6, which shows the relationship between party

2. David Riesman reports that the young in a Vermont village are alienated and apathetic. But they are of a younger age group than those in our sample, and he observes that few individuals in their twenties remain in the village. *Faces in the Crowd* (New Haven: Yale University Press, 1952), pp. 274ff. We should also note that the lack of structural integration among the young is related to a high rate of occupational mobility. S. M. Lipset and Reinhard Bendix, *Occupational Mobility in Industrial Society* (Berkeley and Los Angeles: University of California Press, 1959), pp. 156ff.

identification and voluntary association membership. When we compare those who identify with a political party and those who do not we find that 35 per cent of the Democrats and 46 per cent of the Republicans are members of associations, but 32 per cent of the Independents and only 12 per cent of the "don't knows" are members. The "don't know" response can be interpreted either as symptomatic of a vast indifference to the sphere of politics and government, or as an indication of uncertainty as to where the individual is "located" or "belongs" in the society. The same may be said for at least some of those who identify themselves as "independents"; very often the difference between them and those who respond "don't know" is a greater sensitivity to or concern with what is socially approved. On the other hand, some of the "Independents" are probably individuals who are really alienated from the two major parties. But no matter which of these alternatives describe the "don't knows" and "Independents" it is clear that they are individuals with somewhat looser ties to the society than those who forthrightly declare themselves as Democrats or Republicans.

When we note, however, that 46 per cent of the Republicans belong to associations as contrasted to the 35 per cent of the Democrats who are members the validity of our conclusion seems dubious. But although there is some truth to the old saw that there is no difference between the parties, it is equally true that, since the 1930s at least, the Democrats have been identified as the party which is more willing to innovate and make changes in the social and economic structure, i.e., the Democrats are perceived as more "liberal" than the Republicans. On this basis, then, we may argue that those who identify themselves as Democrats are individuals who feel themselves less committed to the *status quo* and perhaps less involved with the existent social structure. This relatively lesser involvement and commitment would then be reflected in their lower rate of voluntary association membership in the same way that the alienation or indifference of the "Independents" and "don't knows" is reflected.

It is possible, of course, that the difference between Democrats and Republicans is due to class differences between them, but Tables 4:7 and 4:8 offer no evidence in support of this simple explanation. When we compare Democrats and Republicans within each income level, Table 4:7, we see that at the lowest level 28 per cent of the Democrats and 36 per cent of the Republicans join associations, and among the highest income earners 48 per cent of the Democrats and 55 per cent of the Republicans join. However, Table 4:8 presents a deviation from this pattern. Among Democrats with an elementary school education

23 per cent are members, and at the same educational level 33 per cent of the Republicans belong. The percentage of Republican joiners outnumbers that of the Democrats' among those with a high school education, but at the level of the college educated 62 per cent of the Democrats belong and 59 per cent of the Republicans.

An examination of the relationship between occupation, party identification, and membership shows that at the two highest occupational levels there is practically no difference between the membership rates of Democrats and Republicans, but at the other occupational levels the original pattern obtains. Taken in conjunction with the fact that among the college educated the differences between the two groups also tend to disappear, we may speculate that another factor may be involved here. If we assume that voluntary association membership is functional for social mobility and that a larger proportion of high status Democrats are of working class origin than their Republican counterparts, then the higher rate of membership of Democrats of this stripe is a reflection of their felt need for joining associations as a means of obtaining and consolidating a higher status position. On the other hand, to return to our original hypothesis, it may also mean that successful social mobility nullifies the lesser involvement with the existent social structure without at the same time causing a shift in party allegiance.

If socio-economic status does not account for the differences between the two groups, neither does the variable of urbanization. For when we compare those who live in similar urban environments, Republicans have the highest percentage of members and Independents the least. We also see in Table 4:9 that while the rate for Democrats tends to remain constant—approximately a third are joiners—the Republicans' rate increases from 41 per cent in the largest metropolitan areas, to 46 per cent in the smaller metropolitan areas, to 57 per cent in the most urbanized counties. In the least urbanized areas, however, the rate of membership of Democrats tends to increase slightly, 38 per cent are members, and there is a slight decrease in the percentage of Republican joiners.

Race, Nativity, and Membership

In American society, the term "minority group" almost by definition, means individuals who are in the society but not of the society in the same sense as other individuals. We shall first examine the voluntary association membership rates of racial and ethnic groups, and devote the remainder of this chapter to religious minorities.

The statistics reported in Table 4:10 present a confusing picture. According to the AIPO survey results 55 per cent of the whites and 54 per cent of the Negroes are members of associations; that is, there is no significant difference in the membership rates of the two groups. However, the NORC survey results show that more whites than Negroes join associations: 37 per cent of the former are members and 27 per cent of the latter. On the other hand, a third survey undertaken by the Survey Research Center reports that 63 per cent of the whites are members and 69 per cent of the Negroes belong. Moreover, both the AIPO and NORC surveys agree in finding that proportionately more whites than Negroes belong to two or more associations, while the results of the SRC research run in the opposite direction.

Perhaps only because one survey contains any data on nativity is there less of a question here than with the question of race. The results show no difference between native born respondents and those born elsewhere with respect to voluntary association membership. Similarly, the extraction of the parents, whether native or foreign born, seems to have no bearing on the membership rate of their children.

Religion and Membership

The over-all picture of the relationship between religion and membership has two clear facets and an ambiguous one. Table 4:11A shows 58 per cent of the Protestants and 49 per cent of the Catholics as belonging to associations, and Table 4:11B shows 37 per cent of the former and 31 per cent of the latter to be members. In other words, the minority group has fewer voluntary association members. But where the other religious minority stands in this respect is not clear. According to the AIPO survey 52 per cent of the Jews are members of associations, a rate higher than that of the Catholics in the sample but lower than that of the Protestants. On the other hand, 55 per cent of the Jews in the NORC sample belong to associations, a rate higher than those of the other two groups. We are not certain, then, which of the three groups has the highest rate of membership, but we can say with some confidence that Catholics tend to join in fewer numbers than the others.

Since Catholics tend to be concentrated at the lower socio-economic levels it is conceivable that these correlations of religion and membership are spurious. When Catholic and Protestant[3] rates of membership are compared within the same income categories (Tables 4:12A and 4:12B) the general pattern persists. In the AIPO survey sample half the Pro-

---

3. The figures for the Jews are reported in all tables, but since in any given instance the number of cases is small we make no statements about the possible significance of these figures.

testants at the lowest income level and 43 per cent of the Catholics with the same incomes are members. Among those with the highest incomes, 72 per cent of the Protestants and 52 per cent of the Catholics belong to associations. In the other survey 26 per cent of the lowest income Protestants and 28 per cent of the Catholics join associations, but among those earning $5000 a year or more 49 per cent of the Protestants and 38 per cent of the Catholics belong. It would seem, then, the Protestant-Catholic differences in membership tend to become smaller among the lowest income earners.

This is even more apparent when education is taken as the index of socio-economic status. In Table 4:13A, among those with an elementary school education 45 per cent of the Protestants and 44 per cent of the Catholics are members, and Table 4:13B shows that at this level of education 23 per cent of the Protestants and 21 per cent of the Catholics belong to associations. However, in both tables there are significant differences among the college educated comparable to the differences among those with the highest incomes.

A lower rate of Catholic membership is also found in urban communities. Table 4:14A shows that in cities with populations of 50,000 or more 53 per cent of the Protestants and 36 per cent of the Catholics join associations; in the smaller cities 66 per cent of the Protestants and exactly half of the Catholics join. A similar picture is found in Table 4:14B for large and small metropolitan areas. However, in the less urbanized areas the results are less consistent. For example, in the rural non-farm category of Table 4:14A 56 per cent of the Protestants and 58 per cent of the Catholics are members, and the figures of Table 4:14B for the two non-metropolitan areas also show that Protestants do not have higher rates than Catholics. Yet, as can be seen from the statistics of Table 4:14A, in the farm areas once again a higher proportion of Protestants join associations.

When home ownership is taken as an index of urbanization Catholic home owners have higher membership rates than their co-religionists among renters, and home owning Catholics have lower rates than home owning Protestants—a difference between the two groups also found among renters.

Religious Commitment and Membership

Some light may be shed on the question of why Protestants tend to join associations in greater numbers than Catholics by other data on religious attitudes and behavior. The NORC survey asked its respondents how important religion was to them, and the relationship between the importance of religion and membership is reported in Table 4:15. Of those for whom religion is "very important" 38 per cent belong to associations; of those who consider religion to be "fairly important" 33 per cent are members; and of those for whom religion is "not import- ant" 23 per cent belong. Another index of the saliency of religion, church attendance, also shows a correlation with voluntary association membership. For example, in Table 4:16 we see that of those who attend church at least once a week 43 per cent are members, while among those who attend less than once a month or "never" the rate is 33 per cent and 22 per cent respectively. For purposes of discussion we shall label those who feel that religion is "very important" and attend church frequently as being "strongly committed" to their religion.

If strong religious commitment is associated with a high membership rate, then a reasonable expectation is that Protestants are more strongly committed than Catholics. However, this is not the case. Table 4:17 shows that two-thirds of the Catholics go to church at least once a week as contrasted with the third of the Protestants who attend this regularly. Similarly, about 75 per cent of the Catholics (see Table 4:18) feel that religion is very important, while a little over two-thirds of the Protestants stress religion to this degree. In short, despite the fact that a strong commitment to religion is related to a high membership rate, the religious group with the strongest commitment is the group with pro- portionately the least number of voluntary association members.

The situation is neatly summarized in Table 4:19, which compares the membership rate of Catholics and Protestants who attend church at least once a week. Among this select group of religiously minded individuals 46 per cent of the Protestants and 35 per cent of the Catho- lics belong to associations. It seems, then, that a strong commitment to a Protestant religion is associated with a high rate of voluntary associa- tion membership but an equally strong commitment of Catholicism is related to a lower membership rate. This specification of the problem directs our attention to structural aspects of each religion which facili- tate or impede belonging to voluntary associations.

Protestant churches, for example, can be subsumed under the rubric "voluntary association" on two grounds. First, individuals "join" a Protestant church in much the same manner they join associations; this is not true of the Roman Catholic Church. Of more importance, how- ever, is the organizational structure of the churches. In most Protestant denominations power is vested in the congregation, i.e., the minister and other church officials are responsible to the members of the church. The orientations and experience of the Protestant *qua* Protestant would tend to make it relatively easy for him to participate in voluntary associations; such participation would be facilitated by his experience as a Protestant churchgoer. Indeed, it is highly probable that Protestantism was a powerful influence in forming the traditions of voluntary associations.[4]

There is no need to discuss how radically different is the structure of the Catholic Church, but two points will make it easy to grasp how this structure can be dysfunctional for voluntary association membership. According to a Catholic sociologist, one consequence of the structure of the Church is that the clergy tend "to be so bound by the status conditioned view of the office that it becomes impossible to see general problems whole or with detachment: the result is that the initiative of the Catholic layman may be distrusted by the clergy."[5] This hypothesis must be read in conjunction with a central fact of Church structure: "In the power structure of the Catholic Church the appointed priest must exercise a supervisory functional relationship with all parochial societies."[6] Not only is the Catholic Church not a "voluntary association" in the same sense as a Protestant church may be said to be one, but, in addition, if O'Dea's contention that the clergy distrust the initiative of the laity is true, there are crucial Catholic authority figures who do not seem to approve a type of behavior which is the *raison d'etre* of the voluntary association. Moreover, even on the parish level, unlike the situation prevailing in Protestant churches, the position of the priest within the lay organizations of the local church inevitably must result in an organizational experience different from that found in typical voluntary associations. Since the Catholic seems to be more strongly committed to his religion than the Protestant to his, the influence of religion on voluntary association membership in contemporary America is probably more crucial for the Catholic than for the Protestant.

---

4. For example, Kornhauser states: "The rise of religious non-conformity was a major force making for the accommodation of diverse interests in the form of individual rights. Non-conformist groups not only nurtured the idea of individual rights . . . they were *training grounds* and *organized bases* for the exercise of these rights. In particular, they were voluntary associations ready and able to fight for their right to exist . . . More than just the principle, the habits of free association were inculcated by religious dissent." William Kornhauser, *The Policies of Mass Society* (Glencoe, Ill.: The Free Press, 1959), pp. 137f. In Brazil, where Protestant missions have had some success, converts participate extensively in associations. Emilio Willems, "Protestantism as a Factor of Culture Change in Brazil," *Economic Development and Cultural Change,* Vol. 3, No. 4 (July, 1955), 321-33, p. 330. See also Arnold Rose, *Theory and Method in Social Science* (Minneapolis: University of Minnesota Press, 1954), p. 100.

5. Thomas O'Dea, *American Catholic Dilemma: An Inquiry into the Intellectual Life* (New York: Sheed and Ward, 1958), p. 134.

6. Joseph Fichter, S.J., *Social Relations in the Urban Parish* (Chicago: University of Chicago Press, 1954), p. 129.

Previous Research

There are few studies which allow for an easy comparison with our findings on the influence of home ownership and residential stability. A research in Bennington, however, also found that owners had higher membership rates than renters, and those who lived in less than three houses in the course of their residence in the town had higher rates than those who had lived in more than three houses. On the other hand, the total length of time a person was a resident in the town was not related to voluntary association membership. (Scott, 1957) An investigation of an Oregon urban fringe area with a high rate of population growth found through the use of the Chapin Scale that there was a correlation between the length of residence and social participation. In addition, migrants into the area from cities participated more than those who migrated from rural areas. (Martin, 1952) In a Los Angeles suburb long time residents also have higher rates than newcomers, and the longer the commuting distance between home and job the lower the rate of participation in associations. (Scaff, 1952)

Previous research findings on the relationship between religion and membership are, on the whole, congruent with the results reported here. Thus, in Bennington more Protestants than Catholics were members of associations, and in Chicago Goldhamer found that within all age groups Jews had higher membership rates than Protestants and Catholics. (Scott, 1957; Goldhamer, 1942) In New York, however, Komarovsky found no significant differences among the three religions. (Komarovsky, 1946) On the other hand, Wright and Hyman report that another survey of the New York area, as well as one of Denver, found results consistent with those of the NORC survey reported here. (Wright and Hyman, 1958) Hero cites an unpublished research by the American Jewish Committee which found that 91 per cent of the Jews of Memphis, Tennessee, belong to at least one association. (Hero, 1960)

Table 4:1

MEMBERSHIP IN VOLUNTARY ASSOCIATIONS: BY OWNERSHIP AND RENTAL OF RESIDENCE NORC SAMPLE

Per Cent Belonging to	Own	Rent
None	57%	75%
One	22	16
Two plus	21	9
Total	100	100
	(1401)	(964)

Table 4:2

MEMBERSHIP IN VOLUNTARY ASSOCIATIONS: BY OWNERSHIP OR RENTAL AND INCOME NORC SAMPLE

	Own			Rent		
	Under $3,000	$3,000-$4,999	$5,000 or More	Under $3,000	$3,000-$4,999	$5,000 or More
None	64%	62%	49%	85%	73%	63%
One	22	21	24	11	18	19
Two plus	14	17	27	4	9	18
Total	100	100	100	100	100	100
	(369)	(426)	(598)	(316)	(398)	(241)

Table 4:3

MEMBERSHIP IN VOLUNTARY ASSOCIATIONS: BY OWNERSHIP OR RENTAL AND EDUCATION NORC SAMPLE

Per Cent Belonging to	Own Elementary School	High School	College	Rent Elementary School	High School	College
None	71%	53%	37%	86%	72%	53%
One	17	25	26	12	18	22
Two plus	12	22	37	2	10	25
Total	100	100	100	100	100	100
	(511)	(642)	(247)	(352)	(459)	(152)

Table 4:4

MEMBERSHIP IN VOLUNTARY ASSOCIATIONS: BY OWNERSHIP OR RENTAL AND SIZE OF COMMUNITY NORC SAMPLE

Per Cent Belonging to	Metropolitan Area Over One Million Own	Rent	Metropolitan Area Less Than One Million Own	Rent	County Largest Town 10-50,000 Own	Rent	County No Town as Large as 10,000 Own	Rent
None	58%	77%	58%	77%	51%	75%	60%	65%
One	21	15	23	13	23	14	22	25
Two plus	21	8	19	10	26	11	18	10
Total	100	100	100	100	100	100	100	100
	(369)	(362)	(423)	(230)	(268)	(191)	(301)	(166)

Table 4:5

MEMBERSHIP IN VOLUNTARY ASSOCIATIONS: BY OWNERSHIP OR RENTAL AND AGE NORC SAMPLE

	Own		*Rent*	
Per Cent Belonging to	20-34	35+	20-34	35+
None	59%	56%	75%	74%
One	23	22	15	17
Two plus	18	22	10	9
Total	100	100	100	100
	(318)	(1061)	(414)	(535)

Table 4:6

MEMBERSHIP IN VOLUNTARY ASSOCIATIONS: BY POLITICAL PARTY IDENTIFICATION NORC SAMPLE*

Per Cent Belonging to	*Democrat*	*Republican*	*Independent*	*Don't Know*
None	65%	54%	68%	88%
One	20	23	19	9
Two plus	15	23	13	3
Total	100	100	100	100
	(1137)	(623)	(443)	(150)

*"In politics today do you consider yourself a Democrat, Republican, or Independent?"

Table 4:7

MEMBERSHIP IN VOLUNTARY ASSOCIATIONS: BY INCOME AND POLITICAL PARTY
NORC SAMPLE

Per Cent Belonging to	Under $3,000			$3,000-$4,999			$5,000 or More		
	Dem.	Rep.	Ind.	Dem.	Rep.	Ind.	Dem.	Rep.	Ind.
None	72%	64%	83%	71%	58%	67%	52%	45%	62%
One	17	22	14	18	25	18	23	22	23
Two plus	11	14	3	11	17	15	25	33	15
Total	100	100	100	100	100	100	100	100	100
	(347)	(166)	(94)	(399)	(208)	(164)	(383)	(246)	(185)

Table 4:8

MEMBERSHIP IN VOLUNTARY ASSOCIATIONS: BY EDUCATION AND POLITICAL PARTY
NORC SAMPLE

Per Cent Belonging to	Elementary School			High School			College		
	Dem.	Rep.	Ind.	Dem.	Rep.	Ind.	Dem.	Rep.	Ind.
None	77%	67%	83%	61%	52%	68%	38%	41%	52%
One	14	22	12	23	23	22	26	25	23
Two plus	9	11	5	16	25	10	36	34	25
Total	100	100	100	100	100	100	100	100	100
	(457)	(202)	(116)	(541)	(279)	(224)	(138)	(143)	(103)

Table 4:9

MEMBERSHIP IN VOLUNTARY ASSOCIATIONS: BY SIZE OF COMMUNITY AND POLITICAL PARTY IDENTIFICATION — NORC SAMPLE

Per Cent Belonging to	Metropolitan Area Over One Million			Metropolitan Area Less Than One Million			County Largest Town 10-50,000			County No Town as Large as 10,000		
	Dem.	Rep.	Ind.	Dem.	Rep.	Ind.	Dem.	Rep.	Ind.	Dem.	Rep.	Ind.
None	66%	59%	75%	67%	54%	65%	67%	43%	65%	62%	58%	66%
One	19	20	14	18	19	24	15	28.5	20	22	25	21
Two plus	15	21	11	15	27	11	28	28.5	15	16	17	13
Total	100	100	100	100	100	100	100	100	100	100	100	100
	(342)	(189)	(150)	(314)	(144)	(147)	(216)	(129)	(79)	(220)	(159)	(67)

Table 4:10

MEMBERSHIP IN VOLUNTARY ASSOCIATIONS: BY RACE

Per Cent Belonging to	AIPO		NORC		SRC*	
	White	*Negro*	*White*	*Negro*	*White*	*Negro*
None	45%	46%	63%	73%	37%	31%
One	29	36	20	18	30	32
Two plus	26	18	17	9	33	37
Total	100	100	100	100	100	100
	(1802)	(164)	(2139)	(229)	(487)	(54)

*Adapted from Lane, 1960, p. 78.

Table 4:11A

MEMBERSHIP IN VOLUNTARY ASSOCIATIONS: BY RELIGION — AIPO SAMPLE

Per Cent Belonging to	Protestant	Catholic	Jewish
None	42%	51%	48%
One	31	26	35
Two plus	27	23	17
Total	100	100	100
	(1379)	(442)	(89)

Table 4:11B

MEMBERSHIP IN VOLUNTARY ASSOCIATIONS: BY RELIGION — NORC SAMPLE

Per Cent Belonging to	Protestant	Catholic	Jewish
None	63%	69%	45%
One	20	17	25
Two plus	17	14	30
Total	100	100	100
	(1701)	(519)	(71)

Table 4:12A

MEMBERSHIP IN VOLUNTARY ASSOCIATIONS: BY INCOME AND RELIGION — AIPO SAMPLE

Per Cent Belonging to	Under $3,000			$3,000-$4,999			$5,000 or More		
	Prot.	Cath.	Jew.	Prot.	Cath.	Jew.	Prot.	Cath.	Jew.
None	50%	57%	50%	37%	48%	50%	28%	48%	46%
One	31	26	44	32	25	37	28	28	23
Two plus	19	17	6	31	27	13	44	24	36
Total	100	100	100	100	100	100	100	100	100
	(659)	(150)	(16)	(452)	(194)	(46)	(230)	(82)	(26)

Table 4:12B

MEMBERSHIP IN VOLUNTARY ASSOCIATIONS: BY INCOME AND RELIGION — NORC SAMPLE

Per Cent Belonging to	Under $3,000			$3,000-$4,999			$5,000 or More		
	Prot.	Cath.	Jew.	Prot.	Cath.	Jew.	Prot.	Cath.	Jew.
None	74%	72%	45%	65%	76%	62%	51%	62%	37%
One	17	17	22	21	13	19	23	20	29
Two plus	9	11	33	14	11	19	26	18	34
Total	100	100	100	100	100	100	100	100	100
	(540)	(118)	(9)	(592)	(181)	(21)	(549)	(214)	(41)

Table 4:13A

MEMBERSHIP IN VOLUNTARY ASSOCIATIONS: BY EDUCATION AND RELIGION — AIPO SAMPLE

Per Cent Belonging to	Elementary School			High School			College		
	Prot.	Cath.	Jew.	Prot.	Cath.	Jew.	Prot.	Cath.	Jew.
None	55%	56%	67%	37%	49%	52%	21%	44%	25%
One	32	24	13	32	28	33	25	20	55
Two plus	13	20	20	31	23	15	54	40	20
Total	100	100	100	100	100	100	100	100	100
	(518)	(167)	(15)	(643)	(230)	(54)	(207)	(40)	(20)

Table 4:13B

MEMBERSHIP IN VOLUNTARY ASSOCIATIONS: BY EDUCATION AND RELIGION — NORC SAMPLE

Per Cent Belonging to	Elementary School			High School			College		
	Prot.	Cath.	Jew.	Prot.	Cath.	Jew.	Prot.	Cath.	Jew.
None	77%	79%	50%	61%	66%	49%	40%	55%	33%
One	16	11	25	22	20	24	26	21	28
Two plus	7	10	25	17	14	27	34	24	39
Total	100	100	100	100	100	100	100	100	100
	(628)	(189)	(20)	(776)	(253)	(33)	(288)	(75)	(18)

Table 4:14A

MEMBERSHIP IN VOLUNTARY ASSOCIATIONS: BY SIZE OF COMMUNITY AND RELIGION

AIPO SAMPLE

Per Cent Belonging to	50,000 or More			2,500-49,000			Rural Non-Farm			Farm		
	Prot.	*Cath.*	*Jew.*	*Prot.*	*Cath.*	*Jew.*	*Prot.*	*Cath.*	*Jew.*	*Prot.*	*Cath.*	*Jew.*
None	47%	54%	53%	34%	50%	—	44%	42%	—	40%	51%	100%
One	30	28	32	34	25	83	26	25	33.3	37	23	—
Two plus	23	18	15	32	25	17	30	33	66.6	23	26	—
Total	100	100	100	100	100	100	100	100	(99.9)	100	100	100
	(377)	(217)	(18)	(337)	(101)	(6)	(421)	(71)	(3)	(244)	(53)	(2)

Table 4:14B

MEMBERSHIP IN VOLUNTARY ASSOCIATIONS: BY SIZE OF COMMUNITY AND RELIGION

NORC SAMPLE

Per Cent Belonging to	Metropolitan Area Over One Million			Metropolitan Area Less Than One Million			County Largest Town 10-50,000			County No Town as Large as 10,000		
	Prot.	Cath.	Jew.	Prot.	Cath.	Jew.	Prot.	Cath.	Jew.	Prot.	Cath.	Jew.
None	65%	77%	44%	63%	71%	55%	63%	54%	—	64%	53%	—
One	20	14	22	19	17	36	18	23	100	22	23.5	—
Two plus	15	9	34	18	12	9	19	23	—	14	23.5	—
Total	100	100	100	100	100	100	100	100	100	100	100	—
	(387)	(236)	(59)	(474)	(148)	(11)	(371)	(78)	(1)	(406)	(55)	—

Table 4:15

MEMBERSHIP IN VOLUNTARY ASSOCIATIONS: BY IMPORTANCE OF RELIGION* — NORC SAMPLE

Per Cent Belonging to	Very Important	Fairly Important	Not Important
None	62%	67%	77%
One	21	19	10
Two plus	17	14	13
Total	100	100	100
	(1564)	(627)	(116)

*"Quite apart from church going, how important would you say religion is to you—very important, fairly important, or not important at all?"

Table 4:16

MEMBERSHIP IN VOLUNTARY ASSOCIATIONS: BY CHURCH ATTENDANCE — NORC SAMPLE

Per Cent Belonging to	Once a Week or More	1-3 Times a Month	Less than Once a Month	Never
None	57%	63%	67%	78%
One	22	22	20	12
Two plus	21	15	13	10
Total	100	100	100	100
	(883)	(466)	(651)	(287)

Table 4:17

CHURCH ATTENDANCE BY RELIGION — NORC SAMPLE

Attend Church	Protestant	Catholic	Jewish
Once a week or more	33%	66%	14%
1-3 times a month	23	13	17
Less than once a month	32	15	52
Never	12	6	17
Total	100	100	100
	(1666)	(488)	(65)

Table 4:18

IMPORTANCE OF RELIGION BY RELIGIOUS AFFILIATION — NORC SAMPLE

Religion is	Protestant	Catholic	Jewish
Very important	68%	76%	40%
Fairly important	28	21	45
Not important at all	4	3	15
Total	100	100	100
	(1669)	(500)	(67)

Table 4:19

PERCENTAGE OF VOLUNTARY ASSOCIATION MEMBERS
AMONG PROTESTANTS AND CATHOLICS WHO
ATTEND CHURCH AT LEAST ONCE A
WEEK — NORC SAMPLE

Per Cent Belonging to	Protestant	Catholic
None	54%	65%
One	23	19
Two plus	23	16
Total	100	100
	(546)	(322)

CHAPTER V

MEMBERSHIP AND TYPES OF ASSOCIATIONS

The potential significance of the data on the rates of membership is considerably enhanced when they are viewed in relation to information on the types of associations to which individuals belong. In functional terms it makes a difference if we know, to take a limiting case, that only 4 per cent of all voluntary association members are affiliated with organizations which can fall under the rubric, "political and pressure," in addition to our knowledge that between 55 per cent and 36 per cent of all Americans belong to voluntary associations. It follows, then, that a descriptive study of voluntary association membership is rounded off when data on kinds of associations are included in the analysis.

To What Do They Belong?

Table 5:1 gives us an over-all view of the kinds of associations to which individuals belong and the percentage of individuals belonging to each type.[1] The rank order of these types from those with the highest percentages of members to those with the least is: civic and service; lodges and fraternal; church and religious; social and recreational; veterans, military, patriotic; economic, occupational, professional; cultural, educational, alumni; political and pressure.

Membership in both civic and service associations and political organizations may be taken as symbolic of a "community orientation." But Table 5:1 shows that while one type has the highest rank order the other has the lowest. If the functions of voluntary association membership are to link the individual to the community and to play a role in determining attitudes and patterns of behavior in the community, this lack of membership in political organizations is significant. It indicates that his behavior in the community will not be overtly "political"; i.e., his attention will not be explicitly directed at the power structure of the community and he will not see the latter as being immediately relevant to his own situation within the community.[2] Since most of the organizations categorized under the rubrics "civic and service" and

---

1. All the data in this chapter are derived from the NORC survey, 1955. The empirical referents for each category of Table 5:1 and subsequent tables will be found in Appendix B.

2. For an important qualification of this statement see p. 79 below.

"political and pressure" are oriented to the community as a whole, we can put the matter somewhat differently by saying that the distribution of membership between these two kinds of voluntary associations reflects a traditional American suspicion of using political power for achieving community ends.

It should be noted that labor unions are not included in any of these categories. However, 324 (14 per cent) of the respondents belong to unions. Given the structure of American unionism, this does not alter the conclusions about the data reported in Table 5:1. That is, American unions, unlike their European counterparts, are not overtly political groups, and even when the leadership defines itself and the union as a political force its influence is uncertain. To be sure, unions do act as political pressure groups—and so do other organizations, as will be pointed out below—but it is doubtful in the light of the apathy of union members whether this kind of activity is a significant force in orienting the unionized worker to the power structure of the community.[3]

Sex Roles and Voluntary Associations

Voluntary associations are built about specific activities and interests, therefore any differences which appear between men and women in terms of the organization to which they belong will reflect cultural definitions of what is appropriate for men and women respectively. Thus, it is not surprising that Table 5:2,[4] in which the independent variable is sex, shows that more men belong to veterans, military, and patriotic associations than do women. But it is also possible to see that the greater membership of men in lodges and fraternal societies—63 per cent of the membership is male and 37 per cent female—can be explained in the same terms. One of the manifest functions of these organizations is to provide cheap life insurance, burial benefits, etc., and these are functions congruent with the man's family roles.

On the other hand, it is possible to argue that some associations are organized about activities and ends which are culturally defined as appropriate for both sexes. Yet when we examine membership in one type of association which theoretically should exemplify this, church and religious groups, we find that 77 per cent of the members are women

---

3. On the question of apathy see William Spinrad, "Trade Union Participation," *American Sociological Review*, 25 (April, 1960), 237-244.

4. When Table 5:2 is read across toward the totals on the right the figures represent the distribution of the sexes within each type of association. When the table is read down the columns toward the totals at the bottom the figures represent the percentage of members of each sex who belong to each kind of association.

and 23 per cent are men. This means that there is an implicit definition of religion and associated activities as being part of the "woman's world." There is an interesting consistency to this "cultural logic" in light of the fact that women outnumber men in civic and service organizations. Most of the organizations comprising this category have functions which might be termed as "succorance," "supportive," or, more invidiously, "do-goodism"—all implying behavior more congruent with the orientations traditionally associated with the roles of wife and mother. And this, of course, is also congruent with the meaning of activity associated with religion, e.g., the contemporary notion of "charitable works." The greater number of men belonging to civic and service organizations than to church-related groups is probably accounted for by the fact that the former category of associations also contain organizations functional for occupations and careers, e.g., Lions, Kiwanis, etc.

It would seem, then, that the type of organizations to which one belongs is in part determined by the imperatives associated with the sex role.

Age, Social Integration, and Associations

Table 5:3, summarizing the age distribution in different types of associations, points up some interesting differences among the age groups. First, in the civic and service organizations there is a greater percentage of young people than old people; 37 per cent of the membership is between 21 and 34 years of age and only about 10 per cent is 55 or more. However, the opposite occurs among those belonging to lodges and fraternal societies: 18 per cent of the membership falls into the youngest age group and 34 per cent into the oldest.

Both these patterns may be related to the hypotheses we have already elaborated to explain differences in rates among the age groups. The high proportion of young individuals in the civic and service organizations is probably related to the instrumental functions membership in these associations have for occupations and careers. It should be noted that of all those between the ages of 21 and 34 *only 9 per cent are 21-24* years old. This means that the overwhelming majority of the youngest age group are in an age bracket, 25-34 years of age, in which they are beginning to assume full-fledged adult family and occupational roles, i.e., becoming fully integrated into the society. Thus, membership in these associations not only has the aforementioned instrumental functions but is symbolic of the individual's new status in the community. By the same token the sharp drop in the percentage in the oldest group reflects the decreasing saliency of these instrumental functions for those already established in a career or those whose careers have already ended, and is symbolic of the gradual loss of integration with the society characteristic of old age in contemporary America.

At first blush this latter proposition would seem to be contradicted by the percentage of older people belonging to lodges and fraternal societies; of the total membership 18 per cent are in the youngest group and 48 per cent are between 25 and 54. In reality, however, the rubrics themselves indicate support for the hypothesis. That is, "civic and service" explicitly connotes a link between the individual and the wider community, while "lodges and fraternal" connotes a considerably more private sphere of activity. We would hypothesize that the membership rate in the latter type of organization is high, because it offers facilities for interaction and activity of older individuals among themselves. If we recall our previous statement that membership in lodges may be initially motivated by the functions they serve for the imperatives of the male role, it is clear that the same voluntary association may serve different functions for the individual at different stages of life. Thus, the young man may join a lodge to take advantage of cheap life insurance policies, but the same individual as a much older man may use his membership to find a place to meet and interact with others of a similar age status in the society.[5]

However, the functions of associations are related to sex roles as well as age. When the sample is divided into two age groups, less than 35 and over 35, 6 per cent of the membership of church related organizations is composed of young men and 17 per cent of young women. The bulk of the membership is drawn from the older sections of the population, since in these organizations the rest of the membership is made up of 59 per cent older women and 18 per cent older men. On the other hand, there is a tendency for the older men and women to self-select different kinds of associations. Of the membership in lodges and fraternal societies 52 per cent are older men as over against 30 per cent of older women; this is a reversal of the distribution of the sexes in church-related organizations. If it is true that sex roles play some part in determining voluntary association membership, this continuing separation of activities apparent among older persons may signify something more than mere force of convention. Belonging to an association congruent with one's sex role may help the individual to maintain an

---

5. There is, of course, another possibility: as we shall see, there has been a steady decline in membership in this type of organization, and the differences noted above reflect the greater attraction of these associations in an earlier historical period.

identification as male or female at a point in life when retirement from occupational and family roles weakens such an identification.

The Races and Organizations

The comparison of whites and Negroes in Table 5:4 shows some expected patterns and at least one that is a surprise. Given the facts of prejudice and discrimination, it is to be expected that 15 per cent of the whites and only 4 per cent of the Negroes are members of veterans, military, and patriotic associations, and that 17 per cent of the whites and 9 per cent of the minority group belong to associations of a social and recreational nature. Also, in view of the traditionally important role of the church in the Negro community, it is not surprising that 35 per cent of the Negroes belong to church-related associations and 24 per cent of the whites belong to groups of this kind. How central such organizations are in the Negro community can be seen from the fact that more Negroes belong to these than to any of the others, while among whites such organizations rank in third place. On the other hand, while 38 per cent of the whites belong to civic and service associations, almost a third of the Negroes, 31 per cent, also belong to such organizations. If we assume that the bulk of these organizations are all-Negro in membership and have as their "clientele" members of the Negro community, this would indicate that there is a considerable degree of "community orientation" among Negroes.

The one unexpected result in Table 5:4 concerns the rates of membership in political and pressure groups: While 3 per cent of the whites belong to these associations, 13 per cent of the Negroes are members. Normally, we would expect no difference between the races or, if differences did appear, for them to run in the opposite direction. Obviously, given the small number of Negroes upon which the percentages are based, too much cannot be made of this finding, and any conclusions must be highly tentative. So, for example, it is entirely reasonable to assume that the entire Negro sample represented in Table 5:4 is middle class, and that the 13 per cent who are members of political and pressure groups are all members of one organization, The National Association for the Advancement of Colored People. But in view of the fact that only 4 per cent of the entire sample belong to organizations of this sort (Table 5:1), the possibility that over 10 per cent of all Negro voluntary association members may belong to organizations like the NAACP tells us something interesting and important about the Negro community in the United States at the present moment. Our figures may be one indication of a growing self-consciousness in the Negro community; other indications being such events as the Montgomery bus boycott and the lunch counter sit-ins of students. In other words, this may be one of the straws in the wind heralding the real entry of a new force on the American political scene.

Religion, Minority Status, and Organizations

Table 5:5 indicates three areas of difference in the membership patterns of Catholics and Protestants.[6] There is a slight tendency for more Catholics to join veterans, patriotic, and military associations than Protestants: 19 per cent of the Catholics belong to such organizations and 13 per cent of the Protestants join them. Secondly, 39 per cent of the Protestants join civic and service associations and 32 per cent of the Catholics are members. Finally, more Protestants than Catholics also join economic, occupational, and professional organizations—11 per cent of the Protestants and 4 per cent of the Catholics.

These results are extremely suggestive, and they may throw more light on our previous findings on the low rate of Catholic voluntary association membership. One result of a long history of prejudice and discrimination would be the growth of an "avoidance pattern" among members of a minority group; that is, to withdraw from interaction with others and restrict interaction to fellow members of the same group. Therefore, prejudice and its consequences would result in a decline in the rate of participation in the life of the community as a whole. This tendency is further reenforced by a strong central institution like the Catholic Church which by its structure and belief system promotes a high level of group cohesion.

The figures of Table 5:5 are congruent with this hypothesis. We note, first, that Catholics participate less than Protestants in civic and service associations. These are precisely the organizations which link the individual to the community, and they also represent, as it were, the common ground upon which the diverse groups in the community meet and interact with one another. That relatively few Catholics belong to economic, occupational, and professional organizations is probably accounted for, in part, by the fact that fewer Catholics are middle class. But the size of the Catholic middle class cannot wholly account for the difference, since we have previously found that within each class Catholics still had a lower rate than Protestants, particularly in the middle class.

The differences between Catholics and Protestants with respect to

---

6. Again, the number of Jews represented in this table is too small to allow meaningful generalizations.

membership in veterans, military, and patriotic organizations seemingly contradicts the hypothesis, but at least two points must be kept in mind. First, many organizations falling into the category have a wholly Catholic membership, e.g., the Catholic War Veterans. Second, many organizations like the American Legion are fundamentally neighborhood associations. That is, the typical American Legion post, for example, draws its members from a residential neighborhood which is apt to be ethnically and religiously homogeneous, and therefore the Catholic legionnaire is more apt to be interacting with other Catholic legionnaires than with veterans representative of other groups in the society.

The proposition that minority group members have a lower rate of membership in voluntary associations because of prejudice and the "avoidance pattern" is obviously contradicted by the membership rate of the Jews. However, there are three factors present which would tend to make this group a deviate one. First, there is no functional equivalent of the Catholic Church serving to reinforce and maintain a distinct religious identity and a foundation for group cohesion. Second, the group has developed a tradition of voluntary association membership as a result of its history. Finally, the educational level of the group and its rate of social mobility have probably been greater than than of Catholics, and these are factors correlated with high rates of voluntary association membership.

Political Identificaton and Organizations

In previous comparisons of Democrats, Republicans, and Independents we usually found differences among these groups. But as we can see from Table 5:6 there is, with two exceptions, no difference among them in terms of the kinds of organizations they join. About one-fourth of the Democrats and Republicans belong to church and religious organizations—27 per cent and 26 per cent respectively—only 17 per cent of the Independents belong to groups of this type.

Given the American political system, one must talk rather gingerly of the relationship between political parties and "ideology"; that is, one must be cautious in making inferences about "commitment to an ideology" from the mere fact of identification or non-identification with a political party. Nonetheless, if we use the term "ideology" somewhat loosely, we can say that for some, if not all, identification with a political party does imply an "ideological commitment" and identification with a group or stratum in the society. Similarly, membership in a voluntary association with religious affiliations implies some commitment to a religious belief system and identification with a specific social group. One possible meaning of Table 5:6, then, is that those describing themselves as Independents in terms of political party identification tend to be consistent, i.e., they are individuals not only relatively uncommitted to a political ideology but to a religious belief system as well. In short, they may be defined as a relatively alienated and apathetic group in the society. Thus their low rate of membership in voluntary associations of any kind can be seen as both a consequence and a symbol of this alienation.

The other item of interest in this table concerns the membership of political and pressure groups. Of the entire sample 48 per cent of the respondents identified themselves as Democrats, 26 per cent as Republicans, and 19 per cent called themselves "Independents." In all types of associations Republicans tend to be over-represented, and more Republicans than Democrats are members of associations. Yet 60 per cent of the membership of political and pressure groups are Democrats and 31 per cent are Republicans. There are two possible explanations for this. On the one hand, if we take into account that there are more Democrats in the working class than Republicans, this may represent the last vestiges of the Democratic political machines' connections with the urban working class. On the other hand, it may be the result of an interest, awakened during that period, which is more likely to continue among Democrats than Republicans.

Urbanization and Organization

Table 5:7 presents the picture of membership in various organizations by size of community, and it is apparent that differences between communities emerge in four areas of associational activity. First, residents of less urbanized areas tend to have a higher rate of membership in veterans, military, and patriotic associations than do people living in more urbanized communities. In each of the two metropolitan areas 11 per cent and 12 per cent of the respondents belong to these organizations, while in the more urbanized counties 17 per cent belong to them and 19 per cent join in the least urbanized areas. This suggests that the experience of having served in the armed forces, i.e., of living for a period of time in a radically different environment from that of a small town, is a special experience for people in less urbanized areas which may distinguish them both in their own eyes and the eyes of others. Also, it may be another expression of that "integral association between military institutions and rural society."[7]

---

7. Morris Janowitz, *The Professional Soldier: A Social and Political Portrait* (Glencoe, Ill.: The Free Press, 1960), pp. 85.

Membership in organizations of the civic and service types declines among those living in less urbanized areas. In the most heavily populated areas 43 per cent of the respondents join these organizations, and in the smaller metropolitan areas 38 per cent join them. Among those living in the more urbanized and less urbanized counties 25 per cent and 29 per cent respectively are members of civic and service associations. This pattern is congruent with the notion that voluntary associations, especially those of this type, are more important in metropolitan regions. On the other hand, it is more difficult to account for the inconsistency in the results for membership in church and religious associations. Here we find 27 per cent of those in the largest metropolitan areas belong to them, and this rate declines to 20 per cent in the smaller metropolitan areas. But 30 per cent of those living in the more urbanized counties join church-related organizations while 23 per cent of those living in the less urbanized areas belong to them.

Finally, we note that there are differences in the membership rates in economic, occupational, and professional associations. In the metropolitan areas 5 per cent and 8 per cent respectively of the respondents join them, but 11 per cent and 14 per cent respectively of those living in the relatively less urbanized areas are members of these organizations. In the less urbanized regions individuals who would be more apt to be members of organizations of this type, professionals and small businessmen, would not only be a smaller stratum in the community but represent perceptively distinctive orientations and styles of life. Their tendency to belong to associations organized about their occupational and economic interests may be symptomatic of a latent conflict with the rest of the community, especially within the more rural areas.[8]

Within communities differences in membership patterns between owners and renters emerge in two areas of activity. Among home owners 40 per cent belong to civic and service associations, while 33 per cent of the renters join these organizations. Obviously, this may be the result of class differences between the two groups. However, we may also postulate that the economic investment represented by home ownership would motivate a higher level of interest in organizations oriented to "the welfare of the community." Furthermore, the membership rate of owners in this type of association is congruent with our

---

8. This proposition assumes a type of situation like those described by C. Wright Mills, "The Middle Class in Middle Sized Cities," in Reinhard Bendix and S. M. Lipset, *Class, Status, and Power* (Glencoe, Ill.: The Free Press, 1953); and Arthur J. Vidich and Joseph Bensman, *Small Town in Mass Society* (Princeton: Princeton University Press, 1958).

previous hypothesis about the significance of home ownership. We have said that renters are likely to be more mobile individuals and less integrated into the community, and, conversely, owners a more stable group. The difference in the extent of integration into the community each group represents is symbolized by the different rates of membership in civic and service organizations.

Of those belonging to church related organizations there is a slight tendency for owners to have a higher rate than renters: 27 per cent of the owners belong and 21 per cent of the renters are members of such associations. Since owners are likely to be older than renters, and older individuals have a higher rate of membership in associations of this type, the difference between owners and renters probably reflects the more fundamental age difference.

Socio-Economic Status and Organizations

We now turn our attention to the effects of class status upon membership in voluntary associations. Table 5:8 summarizes the relationship between income, as an index of SES, and types of associations. Perhaps the most interesting datum in this table is the rate of membership in civic and service organizations: as income increases the membership rate in this type of organization also increases. The difference between the extremes is striking; 59 per cent of the members of these organizations have an income of at least $5000, and 9 per cent earn less than $3000.

This same pattern is also apparent in membership rates for lodges and fraternal societies. Among the members of these organizations 10 per cent are in the lowest income bracket and 55 per cent in the highest. The rate of membership of the individuals in the upper income levels in these organizations as well as the civic and service ones is probably associated with the instrumental functions such organizations have for occupational and career ends.

Table 5:9 shows, as with income, a correlation between education and membership in civic and service organizations, but here there is an interesting variation. Among those belonging to these associations 10 per cent fall into the lowest educational level and 39 per cent into the highest. However, the majority of the members, 51 per cent, are those with only a high school education. A similar pattern is apparent in the membership of lodges and fraternal associations: 27 per cent of the membership has only an elementry school education; 48 per cent has a high school education; and exactly a quarter of the membership has attended college. This pattern is found again in the membership of church and religious associations, veterans groups, and among those belonging to

social and recreational associations. These findings suggest that education is associated with a particular kind of orientation. A higher rate
of membership in civic and service associations combined with a lower
rate of membership in the other types seems to point to a more "cosmo-
politan" orientation among the college educated as opposed to a more
"local" orientation among the less well educated.

The statistics of membership by occupational status are consistent
with our previous findings for income and education. Thus, the higher
status occupational groups have a higher rate of membership in civic
and service organizations and a lower rate of membership in church-
related associations than those at the lowest occupational levels. The
occupational group with the highest percentage of members in veterans
groups and social and recreational organizations are the skilled workers.

Taking our findings on SES as a whole, the most suggestive are those
on membership in civic and service organizations. We already know
that middle class individuals have a higher rate of membership in all
kinds of voluntary associations than working class individuals. To the
extent that voluntary associations serve as mechanisms for linking the
members of an industrial society to its institutions, one significant conclusion of our over-all findings is that members of the working class
are less likely to be "integrated into the society." Our present results
serve to underline and emphasize this conclusion. Not only are working
class individuals less likely to be members of voluntary associations but,
of those who are, relatively few are affiliated with those organizations
which most directly link the individual and the community or have as
their main orientation that of the community rather than more particular-
istic interests.

There is another point to be considered in this connection. While
we have argued earlier that membership in the organizations falling
into the civic and service category represents a kind of non-political
orientation to the community, especially when compared to that of
membership in political groups, it is nonetheless true that within any
given community the former organizations exercise some influence
within the political structure of the community. Organizations like a
local chamber of commerce or a Parent-Teacher Association do function
as political pressure groups. The fact that such organizations are com-
prised predominantly of middle class individuals means that on the local
community level, at least, the dominant voice is that of the middle class.
Or, to put it more simply, the low rate of working class voluntary association membership, and in this kind of association in particular,
means that this class does not avail itself of one of the means of political

leverage, and as a result is left in a relatively weak position within the power structure.

The membership rate of the working class is obviously related to educational level, but it is important to see that this is only one part of a complex process. A low level of education means a low level of interest in and knowledge of the uses of voluntary associations, and therefore the low rate of membership. But this rate, especially as it applies to membership in civic and service organizations, has the further consequence of maintaining the low level of interest and knowledge of institutionalized means of achieving individual and group ends, i.e., voluntary associations. As a consequence, in conflict situations working class interests cannot be achieved, and this may result in a sense of alienation among members of this class. This sense of alienation, in turn, would result in a reinforcement of initial lack of interest and knowledge of the use of voluntary associations. But, no matter how complex the process which maintains the working class membership rate at a low level, one consequence remains constant: the middle class dominance of the power structure is unimpaired.

Previous Research

A major difficulty in comparing previous work on the types of associations individuals join and the results reported in this chapter is neatly illustrated by Komarovsky's classification of associations: she presents a classification of organizations under twenty headings (including "miscellaneous") while an eight-fold scheme is used here. Nonetheless, some comparisons can be made. In her sample, drawn from the New York metropolitan area, over half the working class association members belonged to "social and athletic clubs" and fraternal organizations. This is congruent with the findings of this chapter, except that a third of the unskilled workers of the national sample belonged to church associations while about 3 per cent of workers surveyed by Komarovsky belonged to associations of this type. The sales and clerical workers in her sample had a similar pattern of membership as those in the national sample, except, once more, that in the national sample a much larger percentage of these white collar people were members of civic associations. Similarly, among businessmen those in the national sample tended to join civic associations more than those caught up by the metropolitan area sample. This difference is probably an artifact of the classification schemes, since Komarovsky's definition of "civic" seems to be much narrower than the one used here. (Komarovsky, 1946)

During their first survey of Middletown the Lynds found that lodges and fraternal groups were declining in importance, and this was confirmed by their second survey. However, during the 1930s fraternal organizations were still important associations for the working class. (Lynd and Lynd, 1929; 1937) Gist presents statistics which bear out the contention that fraternal groups have been declining in importance since the middle years of the 1920s. (Gist, 1940) These two findings are congruent with our finding that younger people have a lower rate of membership in these associations than do older individuals. The high rate of membership of the old in fraternal groups is also confirmed by a study of retired people in two Florida communities. (Webber, 1954) The finding that women tend to join church related associations and men lodges was found to occur in Bennington, Vermont. (Scott, 1957)

In vivid contrast to the American picture is the pattern reported for Sweden. About 10 per cent of the population above 12 years of age belong to athletic associations, and less than 10 per cent to church related groups. In striking contrast with our own society are the almost 50 per cent of all Swedish families who have at least one person who is a member of a consumer cooperative, and 65 per cent of the members of these cooperatives are drawn from the working class as are 55 per cent of the adult members of the athletic associations. Finally, while only 4 per cent of the American joiners in our sample belonged to political or pressure groups, approximately 18 per cent of the Swedish population 12 years of age or older belong to political parties and affiliated youth groups. (Zetterberg, 1960)

Table 5:1

DISTRIBUTION OF VOLUNTARY ASSOCIATION MEMBERS BY TYPE OF ASSOCIATION

Type of Association	Per Cent Belonging*
Veterans, Military, Patriotic	14%
Civic and Service	38
Political and Pressure	4
Lodges and Fraternal	31
Church and Religious	25
Economic, Occupational, Professional	9
Cultural, Educational, Alumni	4
Social and Recreational	16
	(853)

*Percentages do not add up to 100% since any individual may belong to more than one type of association.

Table 5:2

DISTRIBUTION OF VOLUNTARY ASSOCIATION MEMBERS BY TYPE OF ASSOCIATION AND SEX*

Type of Association	Men	Women	
Veterans	22%	9%	
	68%	32%	(120)
Civic	34	46	
	39	61	(322)
Political	3	6	
	33	67	(36)
Lodges	44	23	
	63	37	(265)
Church	13	39	
	23	77	(214)
Economic	13	7	
	63	37	(76)
Cultural	2	6	
	22	78	(32)
Social	14	20	
	39	61	(139)
	(377)	(422)	

*When the percentages are read across toward the base figures in parentheses in the right hand column they represent the distribution of the sexes within each type of association. When the table is read down the columns toward the base figures in the last row the figures represent the percentage of individuals of each sex belonging to each type of association.

Table 5:3

DISTRIBUTION OF VOLUNTARY ASSOCIATION MEMBERS BY TYPE OF ASSOCIATION AND AGE*

Type of Association	21-34	35-54	55 and Over	
Veterans	15%	13%	16%	
	29%	41%	30%	(118)
Civic	49	42	20	
	37	52	11	(308)
Political	4	3	5	
	27	38	35	(34)
Lodges	20	32	40	
	18	48	34	(260)
Church	20	25	31	
	22	45	33	(210)
Economic	9	7	9	
	31	40	29	(65)
Cultural	4	4	3	
	29	52	19	(31)
Social	21	14	14	
	32	**48**	20	(156)
	(234)	(384)	(221)	

*When the percentages are read across toward the base figures in parentheses in the right hand column they represent the distribution of the age groups within each type of association. When the table is read down the column toward the base figures in the last row the numbers represent the percentage of individuals in each age group belonging to each type of association.

Table 5:4

MEMBERSHIP IN TYPES OF ASSOCIATIONS: BY RACE

Type of Association	White	Negro
Veterans	15%	4%
Civic	38	31
Political	3	13
Lodges	31	28
Church	24	35
Economic	9	4
Cultural	4	1
Social	17	9
	(785)	(68)

Table 5:5

DISTRIBUTION OF VOLUNTARY ASSOCIATION MEMBERS
BY TYPE OF ASSOCIATION AND RELIGION*

Type of Association	Protestant	Catholic	Jewish	
Veterans	13%	19%	8%	
	70%	27%	3%	(116)
Civic	39	32	19	
	78	16	6	(313)
Political	4	3	13	
	70	15	15	(34)
Lodges	30	29	54	
	74	18	8	(256)
Church	25	26	33	
	74	20	6	(210)
Economic	11	4	3	
	91	8	1	(73)
Cultural	4	3	3	
	84	13	3	(30)
Social	17	18	8	
	76	22	2	(135)
	(624)	(160)	(39)	

*When the percentages are read across toward the base figures in parentheses in the right hand column they represent the distribution of the religions within each type of association. When the table is read down the columns toward the base figures in the last row the numbers represent the percentage of individuals of each religion belonging to each type of association.

Table 5:6

DISTRIBUTION OF VOLUNTARY ASSOCIATION MEMBERS
BY TYPE OF ASSOCIATION AND POLITICAL
PARTY IDENTIFICATION*

Type of Association	*Democrat*		*Republican*		*Independent*		
Veterans		14%		15%		16%	
	46%		36%		18%		(120)
Civic		37		40		34	
	46		35		17		(321)
Political		5		4		2	
	60		31		9		(35)
Lodges		30		31		34	
	46		34		18		(264)
Church		27		26		17	
	51		36		11		(211)
Economic		8		10		11	
	43		27		20		(76)
Cultural		3		4		4	
	37		37		20		(32)
Social		16		16		16	
	46		34		17		(138)
	(402)		(286)		(140)		

*When the percentages are read across toward the base figures in parentheses in the right hand column they represent the distribution of party identification groups within each type of association. When the table is read down the columns toward the base figures in the last row the numbers represent the percentage of individuals in each political identification category belonging to each type of association.

Table 5:7

MEMBERSHIP IN TYPES OF ASSOCIATIONS: BY SIZE OF COMMUNITY

Type of Association	Metropolitan Area Over One Million	Metropolitan Area Less Than One Million	County Largest Town 10-50,000	County No Town as Large as 10,000
Veterans	11%	12%	17%	19%
Civic	43	38	25	29
Political	5	6	5	*
Lodges	30	34	28	31
Church	27	20	30	23
Economic	5	8	11	14
Cultural	3	4	4	4
Social	14	18	18	16
	(238)	(232)	(178)	(177)

*Less than 1%.

Table 5:8

DISTRIBUTION OF VOLUNTARY ASSOCIATION MEMBERS BY TYPE OF ASSOCIATION AND INCOME*

Type of Association	Under $3,000	$3,000-$4,999	$5,000 and Over	
Veterans	14%	18%	12%	
	22%	40%	38%	(120)
Civic	16	38	47	
	9	32	59	(319)
Political	4	3	5	
	22	22	56	(36)
Lodges	13	23	32	
	10	35	55	(233)
Church	36	24	21	
	31	31	38	(213)
Economic	10	7	10	
	24	24	52	(76)
Cultural	3	5	3	
	16	42	42	(31)
Social	13	19	16	
	17	36	47	(139)
	(181)	(269)	(397)	

*When the percentages are read across toward the base figures in parentheses in the right hand column they represent the distribution of income groups within each type of association. When the table is read down the columns toward the base figures in the last row the numbers represent the percentage of individuals in each income group belonging to each type of association.

Table 5:9

DISTRIBUTION OF VOLUNTARY ASSOCIATION MEMBERS BY TYPE OF ASSOCIATION AND EDUCATION*

Type of Association	Elementary School	High School	College	
Veterans	14%	16%	11%	
	22%	57%	21%	(120)
Civic	16	39	51	
	10	51	39	(322)
Political	3	4	7	
	16	42	42	(36)
Lodges	36	30	28	
	27	48	25	(265)
Church	28	26	21	
	26	51	23	(214)
Economic	12	6	12	
	29	35.5	35.5	(76)
Cultural	3	2	7	
	19	31	50	(32)
Social	13	18	17	
	19	54	27	(139)
	(198)	(426)	(229)	

*When the percentages are read across toward the base figures in parentheses in the right hand column they represent the distribution of education categories within each type of association. When the table is read down the columns toward the base figures in the last row the numbers represent the percentage of individuals in each education category belonging to each type of association.

CHAPTER VI

SOME CONSEQUENCES OF
VOLUNTARY ASSOCIATION MEMBERSHIP

The preceding chapters have been concerned mainly with describing how many people belong to voluntary associations, their social characteristics, and the types of associations to which they belong. In this chapter we shift our attention to another problem: What are the consequences of voluntary association membership?

More concretely, we shall raise the following order of questions and attempt to answer them in empirical terms: Is there a relationship between voluntary association membership and other forms of behavior—in the broadest sense of the term—which also serves to link the individual with his social environment? Is there a relationship between membership and a particular kind of perception of that environment and one's place within it? Does voluntary association membership play a role in determining whether or not an individual knows and understands his community and society? In short, does voluntary association membership "make a difference" in the life of the individual?

This statement of the problem implies a causal relationship between membership and behavior with the independent variable being membership. However, it is clear that this cannot be assumed *a priori* or from a mere inspection of the data; depending upon the particular behavior pattern or attitude under discussion membership may be either a dependent or an independent variable. If it is a causal variable then it must, at least, precede the presumed effect in time. In a great many cases the determination of time precedence is a major problem of survey analysis, and this is especially true of secondary analyses where anticipated difficulties cannot be guarded against by far-sighted research planning.[1] Fortunately, in the present instance when causal inferences are drawn from the observed relationships there is a minimum amount of ambiguity on this point.

"Contact" and "Interest"

The voluntary association is only one link between the immediate life situation of the individual and the broader social environment. What

---

1. For a discussion of the methodological issues involved see Herbert Hyman, *Survey Design and Analysis* (Glencoe, Ill.: The Free Press, 1955), pp. 193ff.

is the relationship between association membership and those other means of contact of individual and society?

Media of communication, e.g., books, newspapers, magazines, etc., are other channels linking individual and community. Since they do not involve direct social interaction these media are not wholly equivalent in function to associations. However, in terms of such functions as disseminating information and contributing to an understanding of the world, books and magazines can be defined as functional equivalents of associations. Even if what is read does not reach beyond the level of a women's magazine, the person is in a somewhat different situation, for better or worse, with respect to the larger world than the person who reads nothing at all. Specifically, then, our concern is with the relationship between the reading of books and magazines and voluntary association membership.

Tables 6:1 and 6:2 represent the first approach to an answer. In the first we cross-tabulate membership and the number of magazines read, and in the second we do the same for the number of hours a week spent reading books. Both tables exhibit the same pattern. Thus, Table 6:1 shows that 51 per cent of the non-members read no magazines at all, while only 23 per cent belonging to two or more associations fall into the category of non-readers. Conversely, only a quarter of the non-members read as many as three magazines, while over half of those belonging to two organizations or more read this many magazines. In Table 6:2 we note that 58 per cent of those belonging to no voluntary associations spend no time reading books as opposed to the 21 per cent belonging to at least two organizations who read no books. Clearly there is some relationship between membership and magazine and book reading.

However, it is very probable that this may be a spurious relationship, since reading depends upon education and the latter is highly correlated with voluntary association membership. Tables 6:3 and 6:4 justify these suspicions, for when we cross-tabulate the number of magazines read and the number of hours spent reading books with educational attainment a strong relationship is apparent. Table 6:4, for example, shows that over two-thirds of those with only an elementary school education or less do not spend any time reading books as opposed to a fourth of those who have attended college.

Therefore, in Tables 6:5 and 6:6 we reexamine the relationships with education held constant. For purposes of simplicity we have divided the variable of membership into members and non-members, and changed the categories of the dependent variables to "none," "few," and "many."

In both tables we note that the original differences between members and non-members remain. In Table 6:5, for example, among those with an elementary school education 69 per cent of the non-members and 51 per cent of the members read no magazines, while at the same educational level 12 per cent of the non-joiners and 26 per cent of the joiners read "many magazines." Among the college educated 19 per cent of the non-members and 12 per cent of the members do not read any magazines at all, and 52 per cent of the non-members read three or more magazines as over against the 68 per cent of the joiners who read this many. Similarly, in Table 6:6 we find at each educational level a greater percentage of non-members than members who do not read books. However, we should note that among the elementary and high school educated more joiners than non-joiners spend "many hours" reading books, but no such difference is present among the college educated.

If we read Table 6:5 in conjunction with Table 6:3 we may see our results from another perspective. In the latter table we see that 65 per cent of those with an elementary school education read no magazines, and 34 per cent of those on the high school level also fall into this category. When we turn to Table 6:5, and direct our attention to the figures for *non-members*, we see that for each of the two educational levels the percentages of those reading no magazines is 51 per cent and 24 per cent respectively. The tendency for the percentage of non-magazine readers to drop among the members is also apparent at the college level, but to a considerably lesser degree.

This pattern is apparent in Tables 6:6 and 6:4. The latter indicates that 69 per cent of those at the lowest educational level spend no time reading books, but Table 6:6 shows 58 per cent of the members with a similar education fall into this category. In the high school group of Table 6:4, 49 per cent spend no time reading books, and this drops to 44 per cent among the members of Table 6:6. The pattern is also found in a much weaker form among the college educated.

What conclusions may be drawn? To recapitulate: reading is taken as an "index" of contact with or interest in the wider community, and thus serves as a link between the latter and the individual life situation. Our problem focused on a possible relationship between this integrative mechanism and that of voluntary association membership. The first conclusion, then, is that such a relationship does exist. Voluntary association membership tends to be part of a configuration which may be labeled "interest in and contact with the environment." More simply, even with the variable of education controlled, association members tend to be linked in greater numbers with the broader community through the reading of books and magazines than non-members.

A second conclusion takes us one step further. Educational attainment is the prime determinant of the amount of reading done, but membership in voluntary associations tends to heighten the effect of education. That is, education plus membership leads to more reading than the same educational attainment with no voluntary association membership.

There are two qualifications to this last statement. The effect of membership on reading is most observable and significant for those with less than a college education, and the effect of belonging to voluntary associations is more pronounced in the reading of magazines than books. In Tables 6:5 and 6:6 the differences between college members and non-members are much smaller than differences between members and non-members at the other educational levels. When these two tables are juxtaposed with Tables 6:3 and 6:4 we note that membership makes less difference in reducing the percentage who do not read at the college level than at the other levels. This point is most easily grasped by comparing the last rows of Tables 6:5 and 6:6. In the former we note that at each educational level more members than non-members read many magazines. In the latter table, however, we note that there is no difference between members and non-members in the spending of "many" hours reading books.

If education is one of the main determinants of interest in the world about one, this interest is additionally supported by voluntary association membership at the lower educational levels; it is more significant there than at the highest level. It is possible that for those with less than a college education a more "active" linkage with the community provided by belonging to voluntary associations may be a pre-condition for establishing other connections. Basically, what we are calling attention to here is the fact that the functions of voluntary associations, insofar as they are related to stimulating interest in or contact with the social environment, may operate differently for the less educated than for the more educated.

The greater correlation of membership with the reading of magazines rather than books for the less educated is the result of the greater similarity of magazines to other mass media. Therefore, if voluntary association membership functions to encourage indirect linkages to the community it is through the mass media of communication that such connections are made.

Social Order and Perception of the Future

We turn now to a more subjective aspect of the individual's relation to the social environment; that is, the way this environment is perceived.

The NORC survey asked its sample the following question: "Many people say that they can live only from one day to another at this time. Do you think this way too, or do you believe you can make plans for the future?" One way of dealing with the meaning of the answers to this question is to say that those who believe in making plans are "optimistic" and those who are sceptical of this possibility are "pessimistic." But these are merely tags which raise more questions than they answer; these feelings arise from more fundamental beliefs and attitudes.

To believe that one "can make plans for the future" implies a basic conviction that the world in which one lives is a predictable and orderly world, that the future is calculable. Put somewhat differently, it is a perception of an orderly and stable world permitting the organization of present behavior for the achievement of future ends. "Pessimism," on the other hand, implies a perception of a lack of order and an unpredictable and incalculable future. What is important to note is that beliefs about the predictability of the future necessarily rest upon the individual's perception and experience of the world in which he exists in the present. This means that our problem concerns the possible relationships between voluntary association membership, present experience, and consequent orientations to the future.

Table 6:7 shows that such a relationship does indeed exist. Of those belonging to no associations 26 per cent view the future as being unpredictable, while 13 per cent of those belonging to two or more associations see the future in this fashion. However, further analysis shows that the greater the educational attainment the higher the percentage of those believing that it is possible to plan ahead.

In Table 6:8, therefore, we control the variable of education and examine the relationship again. We see that for those with the least education the original differences persist—34 per cent of the non-members believe that one can only live from "one day to another" and 25 per cent of the members believe this—but among the high school educated there is a considerable reduction in the size of the difference, i.e., 22 per cent of the non-members feel the future is unpredictable and 17 per cent of the joiners hold this view. In the college group, on the other hand, 9 per cent of the non-members and 8 per cent of the members see the future as unpredictable. This means, in sum, that voluntary association membership makes a difference to a significant degree only among the less educated. In terms of the way we have interpreted the meaning of the question this implies that those who are objectively linked to the wider community, i.e., the joiners, are less likely to experience the world in which they live as lacking order and predictability.

However, the findings for the college educated suggest a somewhat more complex situation. The experience or apprehension of a lack of order in the social environment is not dependent solely upon the situation being in fact unstable; order may exist but it may not be apprehended or perceived. Thus, a person viewing a football game for the first time fails to see that the action at the scrimmage line is anything but random. The prerequisites for seeing order on the football field are the same as for seeing order in society: first, the assumption that order exists; second, some prior knowledge or experience which enables one to detect the order.

In Western society the greater the education the higher the probability of the belief that the world in which one exists, physical or social, is an orderly world,[2] and the more education the greater the likelihood the knowledge needed for detection of the actual order will be acquired. Therefore, what may be objectively the same situation can be experienced differently by two individuals; the essence of order for one will be merely chaos for the other.

What is interesting about our findings, then, is that voluntary association membership seems to mitigate the effects of a lack of education, and this follows from our previous findings and what has just been said. If membership is associated with more time spent reading, then one possible consequence of this is increased knowledge and increased familiarity with the fundamental assumption about order. However, whatever added "increments" of knowledge and experience with the world membership may represent, there are "diminishing returns" once a certain level of education is reached.

If the main line of our interpretation is correct, then we would expect to find, because of the increase in knowledge and contact with the wider community resulting from voluntary association membership, that when low SES members are asked something specific about their possible future status their answers will show less consistency than those of non-

---

2. Since such an assumption is basic to all of Western culture it accounts for the overwhelming percentage of respondents who believe the future is predictable. The response to the question is less a response to an experience with a particular social order than an expression of a fundamental value commitment.

members. The future is, in fact, uncertain, and knowledge makes one aware of how uncertain it is. It is no paradox, therefore, that precisely the individuals who believe the future is predictable will be those showing the least consistency among themselves with respect to expectations of the future.

The NORC survey asked respondents to estimate whether they thought that their incomes five years from now, i.e., the time of the interview, would be higher, the same, or lower than their present incomes. Table 6:9 reports the results in terms of membership. Interestingly enough, there are no differences between members and non-members. However, when we control for income status at the time of the interview, as in Table 6:10, we find a somewhat different picture.

First, when we compare lowest and highest income groups, more non-members in the former category see themselves as having higher future incomes than members, but among those with the highest incomes there is virtually no difference between members and non-members. Second, when we concentrate on the lowest income group alone we note that 15 per cent of the non-members and 22 per cent of the joiners foresee lower future incomes. This contrasts with the 39 per cent of the non-members who see higher future incomes and the 29 per cent of the membership who see themselves earning more in the future. In short, the voluntary association member who has greater knowledge of the world in which he lives is not certain about what the future will be as is the non-member.

Before we leave this problem of the perception of the future we should note the possible relevance of our findings to a more general theoretical issue. One way of conceptualizing our present problem is to use the concept of *anomie.* If the present situation is apprehended by the individual as lacking order this can only mean, individual psychological reasons aside, that social norms are not effectively controlling the behavior of himself and others. Such a perception would represent a psychological consequence of an anomic *situation.* According to Srole's conception of *anomie,* a state of alienation from others, such a perception of the environment represents one dimension of *anomie.* His "Anomie Scale" contains the item, "Nowadays a person has to live pretty much for today and let tomorrow take care of itself."[3] This is but another version of the NORC survey question. The person who is alienated from others will agree with the statement, and therefore our

---

3. Leo Srole, "Social Integration and Certain Corollaries," *American Sociological Review,* 21 (December, 1956), 709-16.

own results tend to confirm this hypothesis. In short, to the extent that a lack of some sort of relationship with others is part of the phenomenon of *anomie,* and to the extent that an apprehension of an unstable environment is one dimension of *anomie,* our own results represent an empirical confirmation of this reasoning.

Knowledge of Community and Society

We have been arguing that membership in voluntary associations leads to greater knowledge, at least in the factual sense, of the social environment. At this point we turn to an empirical test of this proposition.

The AIPO survey of 1954 attempted to discover how much knowledge Americans had of local community organizations engaged in fund raising in the field of health. The survey asked, "Is there a community chest or United Fund (Red Feather) in this community?" Table 6:11 reports the "don't knows" responses by education and membership.

The pattern of these results is clear and unequivocal. At each educational level fewer members than non-members did not know whether a certain kind of organization—and one which functions toward important community ends—did or did not exist in their community.

Our hypothesis talks of the "social environment," and this includes the larger society as well as the local community. We have just seen that membership leads to greater knowledge about the latter, but does it also lead to knowing something on a broader level? Another question of the same survey was: "Do you happen to know the name of the organization that puts on the March of Dimes? What is it?" To know something about the sponsor of the March of Dimes is to know something beyond the level of the local community.

In Table 6:12 we cross-tabulate the number who did not know the sponsor, the number who knew the correct answer, and the "other" responses by membership and education. At the elementary school level 81 per cent of the non-members and 73 per cent of the members did not know the organization sponsoring the March of Dimes. Of those who *thought* they knew the sponsor 14 per cent of the non-members and 21 per cent of the joiners with an elementary school education answered correctly. Among the college educated 40 per cent of the non-members and 36 per cent of the members had no idea who the sponsor was, while of those attempting an answer 57 per cent of the non-members came up with the correct identification and 60 per cent of the members had the right answer. In short, one consequence of voluntary association membership is that it leads to greater factual knowledge of the immediate local environment and of the broader society encompassing it.

Awareness of the World

But knowledge means something more than just a grasp of the "facts." Another implication of the concept of knowledge is an appreciation that the "facts" are aspects of a totality with significance and meaning; "knowledge" implies that one has some awareness of that meaning, or "insight" into the nature of the social environment. Unfortunately, our data do not permit a test of this in relation to voluntary association membership at any profound level, but some approach to the problem is possible.

Another question of the AIPO survey concerned a community problem: "What health problems are particularly bad and need attention in this community?" Table 6:17 reports the number of responses which fall into the general category "can't think of any."

It is obvious that for our purposes the results are somewhat ambiguous. At least two-thirds of the respondents at each educational level respond in this fashion. Of course, this may mean that in the communities in which the respondents lived there were no serious health problems. But another interpretation is possible. Assuming no endemic illness from which all persistently suffer, the question is somewhat ab-abstract and unreal, especially for Americans. Health in our society, except for certain contagious diseases, tends to be thought of as a *private* affair rather than a community or social problem. This would account for the pattern of responses in Table 6:13. It is only among the college educated that a difference between members and non-members is found, but it is only at this educational level one expects that individuals will be able to deal with the "abstractness" of this particular question. If this explanation is valid, then, at the very least, the results do not contradict our hypothesis.

The AIPO survey asked another question which falls along the same dimension of the meaning of knowledge we are concerned with, and it was somewhat less "abstract": "Some people tell us that one of the serious problems in their community is taking care of old people. Is this a problem in this community?" Here the notion of "taking care of old people" is much more specific than that of "health," and it is explicitly labeled as something people consider a problem of the community. It resembles the previous question in that it is concerned with the way the community is functioning with reference to important individual and social needs.

Table 6:14 presents the results in terms of those who responded, "don't know." Here, at least, the pattern is clear. Fewer voluntary association members respond in this fashion than do non-members. The "DK" response is crucial in this instance, because it shows a lack of awareness about "facts," i.e., there are old people who can't work, are in need of economic support, and whose health is failing. Those who don't know whether this is a problem in their community lack awareness of the significance of certain "facts." That this occurred less frequently among those belonging to voluntary associations indicates that membership may indeed promote "social insight."

Participation in Communal Activities

The functions of voluntary associations we have been looking at are somewhat "passive" functions. We have not been thinking of the voluntary association as a means of channeling the individual into active participation within the community. At this point, however, we have to clarify what participation means in this context.

There is, first, participation *within* voluntary associations or participation in community life as a member of a voluntary association. Second, there is participation in the community as a more or less "private individual", i.e., participation in which one's voluntary association membership is irrelevant. Typical of this second kind of participation would be the volunteering of services during the annual Red Cross drive without becoming a member of the local chapter. It is this kind of participation we are concerned with in testing the obvious hypothesis that voluntary association membership is related to community activity.

The AIPO survey asked, "Have you yourself ever taken part in voluntary public service work to help organizations like the Red Cross, the 'March of Dimes,' the Boy Scouts, and things like that?" The responses were coded in terms of the number of organizations to which the individual offered his services, and this provides a rough measure of communal activity.

Our hypothesis is clearly supported by the results found in Table 6:15. When we control for education we see that among the least educated 91 per cent of the non-members and 81 per cent of the joiners engaged in no communal activity at all. At this educational level 1 per cent of the non-members and 5 per cent of the members participated in the work of at least two organizations. When non-joiners and joiners among the college educated are compared we find that 51 per cent and 34 per cent respectively participated in no communal activity. And of those who worked with two or more organizations 17 per cent did not belong to voluntary associations and 41 per cent were joiners. The findings have some obvious bearings on the problem of the role of associations in contemporary American society. However, since we shall examine the significance of all our findings in terms of this problem in the next chapter, we shall postpone a discussion of the meaning of these results until that point.

Previous Research

There has been a fair amount of research upon the consequences of social participation and voluntary association membership for attitudes and behavior. We shall concentrate on those most readily comparable with the problems examined in this chapter.

Our basic assumption that voluntary association membership is part of a "configuration of linkages" to the community has been stated as an empirical generalization in a somewhat different fashion by two Finnish sociologists. Allardt and Pesonen state that their researches show a "cumulativeness of activity" within behavior systems, i.e., there is a positive correlation between association membership and other forms of social participation, and membership is correlated with the reading of books and periodicals, listening to the radio, etc. (Allardt and Pesonen, 1960)

If we take voting as analogous in the political sphere to helping the Red Cross fund drive without being a member of the organization, then the hypothesis that association membership is associated with other forms of social participation is confirmed by other studies. In a West Virginia community members of associations tended to vote in greater numbers than non-members. (Maccoby, 1958) In a Michigan city and its fringe area a greater percentage of joiners both registered and voted than did those who did not belong to associations. (Zimmer and Hawley, 1959b) Similarly, in a Massachusetts community the same relationship between voting and membership was found. (Hastings, 1956) Finally, Lipset cites a study by Linz, who found in West Germany that joiners in all classes were more interested in politics, voted in greater numbers, read more newspapers, and listened to radio more than did those who did not belong to associations. (Lipset, 1960)

Table 6:1

NUMBER OF MAGAZINES READ BY VOLUNTARY ASSOCIATION MEMBERS — NORC SAMPLE

	Number Organizations Belonged to		
Number of Magazines	*None*	*One*	*Two or More*
0	51%	31%	23%
1	12	12	6
2	13	16	14
3 or more	24	41	57
Total	**100**	**100**	**100**
	(1495)	(464)	(379)

Table 6:2

TIME SPENT READING BOOKS BY VOLUNTARY ASSOCIATION MEMBERS — NORC SAMPLE

	Number Organizations Belonged to		
Hours per Week	*None*	*One*	*Two or More*
0	58%	45%	21%
1-2	20	25	17
2-5	11	15	10
6 or more	11	15	52
Total	**100**	**100**	**100**
	(1489)	(464)	(608)

Table 6:3

NUMBER OF MAGAZINES READ: BY EDUCATION — NORC SAMPLE

Number of Magazines	Elementary School	High School	College
0	65%	34%	15%
1	11	13	9
2	9	16	15
3 or more	15	37	61
Total	100 (851)	100 (1094)	100 (400)

Table 6:4

TIME SPENT READING BOOKS: BY EDUCATION — NORC SAMPLE

Hours per Week	Elementary School	High School	College
0	69%	49%	25%
1-2	17	26	25
2-5	6	13	20
6 or more	8	12	30
Total	100 (838)	100 (1090)	100 (395)

Table 6:5

NUMBER OF MAGAZINES READ: BY EDUCATION AND VOLUNTARY ASSOCIATION MEMBERSHIP — NORC SAMPLE

Number of Magazines	Elementary School		High School		College	
	Non-Member	Member	Non-Member	Member	Non-Member	Member
None	69%	51%	41%	24%	19%	12%
Few (1-2)	19	23	31	27	29	20
Many (3+)	12	26	28	49	52	68
Total	100	100	100	100	100	100
	(654)	(194)	(668)	(423)	(171)	(226)

Table 6:6

TIME SPENT READING BOOKS: BY EDUCATION AND VOLUNTARY ASSOCIATION MEMBERSHIP — NORC SAMPLE

Hours per Week	Elementary School		High School		College	
	Non-Member	Member	Non-Member	Member	Non-Member	Member
None	73%	58%	52%	44%	30%	21%
Few (1-5)	21	27	38	40	40	49
Many (6+)	6	15	10	16	30	30
Total	100	100	100	100	100	100
	(651)	(187)	(667)	(423)	(172)	(223)

Table 6:7

PREDICTABILITY OF THE FUTURE: BY VOLUNTARY ASSOCIATION MEMBERSHIP — NORC SAMPLE

| | *Number Associations Belonged to* | | |
	None	*One*	*Two or More*
One day to another	26%	19%	13%
Plan ahead	74	81	87
Total	100	100	100
	(1474)	(468)	(375)

Table 6:8

PREDICTABILITY OF THE FUTURE: BY EDUCATION AND VOLUNTARY ASSOCIATION MEMBERSHIP — NORC SAMPLE

| | *Elementary School* | | *High School* | | *College* | |
	Non-Member	*Member*	*Non-Member*	*Member*	*Non-Member*	*Member*
One day to another	34%	25%	22%	17%	9%	8%
Plan ahead	66	75	78	83	91	92
Total	100	100	100	100	100	100
	(635)	(195)	(666)	(422)	(171)	(226)

Table 6:9

PERCEPTION OF FUTURE INCOME: BY VOLUNTARY ASSOCIATION MEMBERSHIP — NORC SAMPLE

Future Income Will Be	Non-Member	Member
Higher	42%	42%
Same	37	36
Lower	11	15
Don't Know	10	7
Total	**100**	**100**
	(1510)	(846)

Table 6:10

PERCEPTION OF FUTURE INCOME: BY PRESENT INCOME AND VOLUNTARY ASSOCIATION MEMBERSHIP — NORC SAMPLE

Future Income Will Be	Under $3,000 Non-Member	Member	$3,000-$4,999 Non-Member	Member	$5,000 and More Non-Member	Member
Higher	39%	29%	50%	46%	49%	52%
Same	46	49	39	41	38	32
Lower	15	22	11	13	13	16
Total	**100**	**100**	**100**	**100**	**100**	**100**
	(443)	(160)	(510)	(246)	(412)	(372)

Table 6:11

KNOWLEDGE OF COMMUNITY ORGANIZATIONS: BY EDUCATION AND VOLUNTARY ASSOCIATION MEMBERSHIP — AIPO SAMPLE

	Elementary School		High School		College	
	Non-Member	Member	Non-Member	Member	Non-Member	Member
Don't Know	31%	21%	20%	9%	13%	10%
	(405)	(328)	(392)	(562)	(76)	(209)

Table 6:12

KNOWLEDGE OF MARCH OF DIMES SPONSOR: BY EDUCATION AND VOLUNTARY ASSOCIATION MEMBERSHIP — AIPO SAMPLE

	Elementary School		High School		College	
	Non-Member	Member	Non-Member	Member	Non-Member	Member
"No"	81%	73%	59%	48%	40%	36%
Correct Answer	14	21	34	46	57	60
Other	5	6	7	6	3	4
Total	100	100	100	100	100	100
	(405)	(327)	(389)	(556)	(76)	(206)

Table 6:13

PERCEPTION OF COMMUNITY HEALTH PROBLEMS: BY EDUCATION AND VOLUNTARY ASSOCIATION MEMBERSHIP — AIPO SAMPLE

	Elementary School		High School		College	
	Non-Member	Member	Non-Member	Member	Non-Member	Member
Can't Think of Any	75%	75%	71%	68%	72%	64%
	(405)	(328)	(392)	(562)	(76)	(209)

Table 6:14

PERCEPTION OF A SERIOUS COMMUNITY PROBLEM: BY EDUCATION AND VOLUNTARY ASSOCIATION MEMBERSHIP — AIPO SAMPLE

	Elementary School		High School		College	
Old Age as a Problem	Non-Member	Member	Non-Member	Member	Non-Member	Member
Don't Know	22%	17%	19%	13%	21%	11%
	(405)	(328)	(392)	(562)	(76)	(209)

Table 6:15

PARTICIPATION IN VOLUNTARY PUBLIC SERVICE WORK: BY EDUCATION AND VOLUNTARY ASSOCIATION MEMBERSHIP — AIPO SAMPLE

No. of Organizations Worked With	Elementary School		High School		College	
	Non-Member	Member	Non-Member	Member	Non-Member	Member
0	91%	81%	79%	54%	51%	34%
1	8	14	14	26	32	25
2 or more	1	5	7	20	17	41
Total	100	100	100	100	100	100
	(405)	(328)	(392)	(562)	(76)	(209)

CHAPTER VII

MEMBERSHIP AND THE FUNCTIONS OF ASSOCIATIONS

The introductory remarks to this study pointed out that a description of voluntary association membership in the United States was important, because of the significant role played by associations in a liberal, democratic society. In this concluding chapter we return to this theme in an attempt to assess the significance of the findings of this research.

The Citizenship Functions

It is axiomatic that the preservation of a stable political democracy demands an "informed citizenry," and this means a citizenry which not only has the necessary factual knowledge for making rational decisions but also insight into and understanding of the social environment. The voluntary association is supposed to contribute to both ends; indeed, Arnold Rose is even more emphatic in suggesting that association membership presents the individual with the opportunity to become aware of "how processes function . . . how things are done" in a democratic society.[1] This implies, by logical extension, that members can learn how to use the social and political mechanisms available for the achievement of their goals. Extending this line of thought still further, we can say that the association has consequences for leadership in the society. Knowledge, insight, awareness of social mechanisms, and ability to manipulate them must be considered among the minimum requirements for leadership; therefore association membership helps in the socialization of leaders.

The data presented in the last chapter support the notion that voluntary associations do contribute to factual knowledge and insight. The spread of formal education, however, has diminished the importance of associations in this context: the greater the level of education the smaller the observed differences between members and non-members. In other words, in a society like our own the significance of the voluntary association in maintaining an "informed citizenry" tends to decrease.

Our data provide less direct evidence for assessing the validity of the notion that associations help teach "how things are done." Infer-

---

1. *Theory and Method in the Social Sciences* (Minneapolis: University of Minnesota Press, 1954), p. 69.

111

entially, however, the data do suggest that it is an overstatement. Knowledge of the social and political mechanisms can be enhanced only if association membership actually results in introducing the individual into the mainstream of social and political life. Yet many associations to which individuals belong—social and recreational, church and religious, lodges and fraternal, cultural—tend to be tangential to those areas of life in which it would be possible to gain some knowledge of "how processes operate," and it is doubtful that many of the remaining associations can really function toward this end. But even assuming they can, the number who belong to them is small, and therefore the significance of associations in performing this function is correspondingly less.

It is possible to argue, of course, that almost all associations in our society are democratic, and even a hobby club reproduces in miniature the processes of the larger society. The validity of the assumption that experience in the microcosm fits one to understand and interact in the macrocosm is doubtful, but there are more pragmatic grounds for scepticism here. Most organizations are "democratic" in name only; for the American Medical Association as well as the local social and athletic club "oligarchical" is a more apt descriptive term. Membership and participation within these organizations hardly leads to the type of experience functional for the survival of political democracy within the larger society.

Yet even if we concede, in spite of all this, that there is still some likelihood that learning "how things are done" will result from association membership it is still necessary to face the final irony. When the size of a social structure increases, be it an association or a community, there is an increasing difficulty in achieving and maintaining the substantive rationality implied in the phrase "knowledge of how things are done." This suggests that the citizen of a small community, regardless of whether he is an association member or not, has a better opportunity of achieving substantive rationality, at least as far as his local community is concerned, than does the resident of a metropolis. But it is precisely in the metropolitan areas that the level of membership in associations is lowest. In short, as with the variable of education, that portion of the society which theoretically can benefit most from membership is least represented in the rolls of voluntary associations.[2]

---

2. This conclusion applies even more forcefully to the working class. However, the working class and the functions of associations will be discussed in a separate section. See p. 118 below.

The slow erosion of democratic processes which is found in many voluntary associations is due in part to the interrelated factors of size and bureaucratization,[3] but the latter, when seen from another perspective, may also have functional consequences. In a society which has passed through the "organizational revolution" adequate leadership presupposes certain administrative and social skills appropriate to bureaucratic contexts. That is, the contemporary leader needs knowledge of and insight into bureaucratic processes as well as more general and diffuse processes. To the extent that voluntary associations are bureaucratic structures, it is possible to hypothesize that they serve as valuable training grounds for potential leaders in wider spheres of action. This may be true in some cases, but the other side of the coin carries greater weight. Leadership in voluntary associations may be denied to those who have not already acquired the necessary bureaucratic skills and knowledge elsewhere; instead of being the training ground for leaders, associations become the contexts for the further exercise of skills learned in other spheres.

It would seem, then, that the citizenship functions of voluntary associations are somewhat irrelevant because of three factors: those who would benefit most from membership are not members; the spread of formal education; and the structure of associations themselves. However, two further points must be added to this conclusion. First, it is a conclusion about associations in contemporary America. In earlier stages in our history the voluntary association may have played a more critical role in maintaining an "informed citizenry." To recognize that the functions of voluntary associations may vary in importance depending upon the stage of development of the society is particularly important once we lift our sights to observe other societies. So, for example, conclusions about associations in the United States today may be irrelevant for an understanding of their role in, say, Israel or Ghana.[4]

Secondly, while the educational functions of voluntary associations may be diminishing in importance, this should be seen in its proper perspective. For the highly educated, knowledge, insight, and awareness of "how things are done" are not dependent upon membership, but this does not mean that the latter play no role at all. For example, membership may not automatically mean the learning of how social mechanisms operate, but it is hard to deny that the association member has a better

---

3. Bernard Barber, "Participation and Mass Apathy," in Alvin W. Gouldner (ed.), *Studies in Leadership* (New York: Harper & Bros., 1950), pp. 477-504.
4. Kenneth Little, "The Role of Voluntary Associations in West African Urbanization," *American Anthropologist*, 59 (August, 1957), 579-96.

opportunity to learn or to supplement his understanding of how things are done than the non-member. In short, while there are grounds for justifiable skepticism about how much associations contribute today to the growth of an "informed citizenry," this skepticism should not blind us to a certain continuing utility of the association for the achievement of this end.

Group Interests and Voluntary Action

By definition, a democratic structure presents the most opportunities for individual and group interests to be satisfied, but an essential prerequisite for succesful action is the formation of relatively strong associations which permit groups to exercise their influence and power. Voluntary associations have traditionally functioned as "interest groups," and it is through affiliation with them that the individual has sought to enhance and protect his own interests.

It is obvious from our findings that not all groups in the society are equally equipped in terms of organization to attain their interests. So, for example, in urban communities the fact that home owners have higher rates of membership in associations means that they are potentially, if not actually, in a better position to protect their interests than are renters when there are conflicts over such programs as urban renewal, public housing, etc. There is more involved here than simply disproportion in the distribution of power resources between two groups. The example suggests a complex relationship between the membership rate of home owners, the low rate of membership in metropolitan areas, and the many problems faced by large cities. These problems, it is generally agreed, are not being adequately dealt with by the society; that is, there are few adequate measures being developed for coping with such problems as education, mass transit, housing, etc.

Because many of these problems are either inherently area problems, or because effective "solutions" depend upon resources beyond those commanded by local communities, an adequate approach to them must assume that the state and federal governments must be involved in any ultimate practical measures. There are precedents for the assumption of responsibility by the federal government in dealing with area problems, e.g., land reclamation projects, hydroelectric power projects, etc. But urban problems are not defined in the same manner as are those which affect rural and agricultural interests. The lag in the emergence of a similar kind of orientation to metropolitan area problems may be due to the lack of organizations representing distinctly urban interests, and a general lack of organizational experience hampering an effective use of the institutional means for exercising influence and power. On the other hand, when we consider specific kinds of problems, e.g., education, urban renewal, it may not be a lack of organization, but, as it were, an imbalance in organization. The better organization of home owners, for example, may impede the development of effective programs of urban renewal, because owners are more likely to see such programs as injuring their interests. Therefore, if some segments of the population have higher rates of membership than others, it means that not only will certain groups' interests be slighted but the lack of significant representation of all interests will result in dysfunctional consequences for the community as a whole.

However, the situation is even more complicated than this suggests. If associational life is at a low ebb in metropolitan areas it is, in fact, related to the practical elimination of a critical function once performed by voluntary associations. De Tocqueville underlined this function when he reported, "If a stoppage occurs in a thoroughfare and circulation of vehicles is hindered, the neighbors immediately form themselves into a deliberative body; and this extemporaneous assembly gives rise to an executive power which remedies the inconveniences before anybody has thought of recurring to preexisting authority superior to that of the persons immediately concerned."[5] In the past voluntary associations have performed those functions that government was unwilling or unable to perform; as more and more of those functions have been assumed by government—ironically enough, often as a result of the activities of voluntary associations acting as pressure groups—a powerful force sustaining associations and motivating membership has been sapped of strength.

It is now an axiom of American political theory that the decline of the political party on the local level is significantly related to the growth of government policies symbolized by the term "welfare state." But the growth of the welfare state has probably affected other associations in the same manner not only by taking over some of the functions of these associations but also because it is now generally thought that certain functions *should* be assumed by the state rather than left in the hands of voluntary associations. Thus, the "obstructed thoroughfare" today will not be attacked by private action but left to the duly constituted agents of the state. Moreover, given the complexity of life in a highly urban community, it is doubtful whether the association could

5. Alexis de Tocqueville, *Democracy in America* (New York; Vintage Books, 1954), Vol. 1, p. 198.

actually function as effectively as a government agency. This means that the decline of associations is related to the fact that the structure of contemporary society robs associations of an important *raison d'etre.*

But the decline of associations still has dysfunctional consequences in spite of the acceptance of the welfare state. For, as we have seen, there are still areas of action to which the state is relatively insensitive, and when this is combined with the active opposition of some highly organized segments of the community certain responsibilities are not assumed and problems persist. In addition, while there are areas in which associations cannot meet certain basic needs of the community, there are some in which associational activities can still be effective. Thus, the recent growth in cooperative housing ventures shows that there may be a role for the voluntary association even in our complex society.

Opinion

The observation that the assumption of responsibilities by the state was in part due to the pressure exerted by voluntary associations implies that one of the functions of voluntary associations concerns social change and social reform.[6] A further conclusion from what has been said above, then, is that this function too has been weakened in contemporary America. This is confirmed by our survey findings: not only is less than five per cent of the population formal members of political parties but there is also a low rate of membership in those associations manifestly oriented to political and social problems; organizations whose actions might tend to culminate in social innovation or reform.

The weakness of the association in this area is closely related to another function traditionally assigned to associations—the crystallization of opinion. Reform or change in democratic societies is usually the result of a resolution of conflicting group interests. The association as perceived by Tocqueville, for example, played an important part in this process by organizing those with common interests, thus keeping them aware of their interests with respect to given situations and making it possible for a more or less unified opinion to emerge. Once group opinion formed, organizations made it easier to influence others, and new or innovative opinions could be legitimated, in part, by associations, since the mere fact of being supported by an organized group lends a certain status to the new opinion.[7] The voluntary association as a

---

6. Rose says this is one of the primary functions of associations. *Op. cit.,* p. 51.

7. De Tocqueville, *op. cit.,* Vol. II, p. 117.

means of disseminating and influencing opinion was closely linked by De Tocqueville with other means of communication and persuasion: "Newspapers make associations, and associations make newspapers."[8]

At an earlier period in history the association and the newspaper may have functioned as alternative means of communication and persuasion, and between them all segments of the population may have been reached. Such a view is impossible to sustain today, since those who are the greatest users of the means of communication, the middle class, also form the bulk of the membership of associations. However, there is still an interesting interplay between associations and the communication media which has consequences for the role of associations as innovative mechanisms.

The important means of communication today are those which define their potential audience as the entire society rather than one segment of it. If the mass media of communication are to attain their ideal goal they must reflect the largest possible range of opinions and interests, and their ability to secure mass audiences is in some way related to the strength of associational life. When those with common interests are members of associations there is a reenforcement of the salience of the interests and a crystallization of opinion reflecting these interests. Since there are conflicting interests in a society, a single mass medium cannot really reflect or incorporate all interests; inevitably part of its audience must be alienated. The greater the crystallization of interest and opinion, the larger the size of the audience which may potentially be alienated.

Obviously, no matter what the level of associational life is, the mass media always run the danger of alienating parts of their audiences. One way out of this difficulty is to structure the contents of communication so that real differences in interests are blurred; contents are structured in such a fashion that potential antagonisms stemming from specific value commitments are not stimulated.[9] While this eliminates conflict between the medium and its audience, it also eliminates a functional consequence of conflict: an awareness of common interests and group

---

8. *Ibid.,* p. 120.
9. "The Federal Communications Commission . . . is the source of an enlightening tidbit on the trials of being a writer for video. As a guide in the production of 'Tales of the Texas Rangers,' the sponsor, General Mills Inc., said no material in its script should be offensive 'either directly or by inference to an organized minority group, lodge or other organization, institutions, residents of any state or section of the country, or a commercial organization of any sort.

" 'This shall be taken to include political organizations, fraternal organizations, college and school groups, labor groups, industrial, business, and professional organizations, religious orders, civic clubs, memorial and patriotic societies, philanthropic and reform societies, athletic organizations, women's groups, etc.' " *The New York Times,* October 24, 1960, p. 55.

cohesion—both prerequisites for strong associations. In short, the situation we have been describing can most aptly be summarized by standing De Tocqueville on his head: the weakness of associations makes for mass media, and mass media make for the weakness of associations.

But the association may still play a role in the dissemination of opinion; political opinion is spread most pervasively and persuasively through personal contact.[10] Therefore, voluntary associations, from those manifestly oriented to political and social issues to the hobby club, as the context for personal interaction may serve as channels for the spread of opinions. Yet if this is the case we should remember that this is not the same thing as saying that the association is an important focus of the crystallization of opinion. The latter concept implies that opinion arises out of the interaction of those with common interests; the association conceived as a channel for the spread of opinion implies that the "opinion" has not originated in the interaction of association members. In all probability the "opinion" has been derived from attention to one of the mass media.

Assuming that this accurately describes the situation which obtains today, then associations are not likely to be the breeding grounds for ideas which lead to innovation and reform, and they cannot serve as means of effectively legitimating innovative ideas and ideologies. For if the association has come to be only a channel for the spread of "opinion" then it is quite likely that the association *qua* association is not an important reference group for the formation of members' opinions.[11]

"Human Fellowship"

So far we have been discussing more or less manifest political functions of voluntary associations, but associations have other ends as well. One of the most important of these is that of bringing individuals into interaction with one another; what Rose calls the promotion of "human fellowship."[12] This function of associations is usually stressed, since one of the consequences of urbanization and industrialization is supposed to be a greater isolation of individuals. Recent reasearch tends to cast

---

10. Paul F. Lazarsfeld, Bernard Berelson, and Hazel Gaudet, *The People's Choice* (New York: Duell, Sloan and Pearce, 1944), pp. 150ff.

11. This does not mean that associations do not influence the formation of opinion; rather their influence is declining relative to other sources of influence. On the role played by associations in the influencing of opinion see Howard Freeman and Morris Showel, "Differential Influence of Voluntary Associations," *Public Opinion Quarterly,* 15 (Winter, 1951-52), 703-714.

12. Rose, *op. cit.,* p. 103.

some doubt on this assumption. Even in highly urbanized communities there are many neighborhoods in which the rate of informal interaction among neighbors is high.[13] Moreover, even in a society with a conjugal family structure there is a high rate of interaction among members of the extended family.[14] But while it may be a mistake to see a low rate of membership as being correlated with social isolation, it would be equally mistaken to ignore some consequences similar to those which follow from social isolation.

Throughout this study we have talked of membership as being indicative of social integration, i.e., affiliation with an association acts as a bridge between the immediate life situation of the individual and the wider community and society. The individual whose interaction with others is limited to neighbors and relatives is one who is living within a relatively *narrow world.* To be sure, the association is also in some respects a narrow world in that it tends to be homogeneous with respect to class. Nonetheless, the membership of an association is apt to be more heterogeneous. In other words, association membership provides opportunities for broader social experiences if only because of this heterogeneity. This is important in terms of three consequences.

The first has to do with the quality of an individual's life. The basic assumption is that the greater the diversity of social experiences open to individuals the greater the chances for an "improved" quality of life. The essential idea may be expressed in somewhat different terms: when the range of life is broad rather than narrow there are greater opportunities for what the psychologists call "self-realization."

A second consequence is that a greater diversity of experience may contribute to raising the threshold of tolerance of ambiguity. This is of particular relevance to a contemporary political democracy, since almost by definition ambiguity and uncertainty are pervasive within such a society. Here voluntary association membership may act in the same way that education does in promoting a greater tolerance for the ambiguities entailed in living in a modern society.[15]

A third consequence can perhaps best be understood by referring back to one of our empirical findings. One of the groups with a low rate of membership is the Catholics, and it is interesting to note that within

---

13. See, for example, Scott Greer, "Urbanism Reconsidered: A Comparative Study of Local Areas in a Metropolis," *American Sociological Review,* 21 (February, 1956), 19-25.

14. This is true of all social classes. Morris Axelrod, "Urban Structure and Social Participation," *ibid.,* 13-19.

15. In this connection see S. M. Lipset, *Political Man* (Garden City: Doubleday and Co., 1960), pp. 97ff.

the group today there is a great deal of self-criticism having to do with an alleged "defensiveness" and the quality of Catholic education.[16] In addition, the charge has been made that there is a "relative paucity of Catholic writing and participation in such areas as community relations, urban planning, religious pluralism, the ethics of mass communication and civil liberties."[17] Since Catholics tend to be non-joiners, have a high rate of church-going, and a high proportion of their numbers are educated exclusively in Catholic schools, it is fair to say that the members of this group tend to inhabit a rather more restricted world than members of other religious groups. What is important here is that the problems pinpointed by Catholic critics may in part result from this restrictive life experience of Catholics; that is, not only does the individual suffer from living in a narrow world but the group too experiences dysfunctional consequences. This, in turn, has another result: whatever Catholics can contribute to the society in terms of their sub-cultural religious heritage is being lost to the society. In other words, when individuals and groups live within relatively narrow worlds their capacities tend to be less developed, and this represents a loss to the society which in some measure depends for its survival on the maximum development of individual capacities and potentials.

The Socialization Function

Discussions of voluntary associations in the American context have tended to ignore what has probably been an important goal of associations in European contexts, i.e., a socialization function.[18] So, for example, the Social-Democratic parties of Germany and Austria have traditionally nurtured extensive "youth movements"—voluntary associations built about the interests of young people and dominated by the ideology of the party. Such youth organizations, of course, are a well known feature of totalitarian societies as well. Obviously, the manifest function of these organizations is to indoctrinate the young, the future members of the party, and maintain ideological continuity.

The functional equivalents of these associations are unknown in the United States. Associations which have young people as their members are either scout groups of one kind or another or spontaneously formed "social and athletic clubs" of urban teenagers. These groups differ

16. For a review of the Catholic literature on this problem as well as a sociological analysis: Thomas F. O'Dea, *American Catholic Dilemma: An Inquiry into the Intellectual Life* (New York: Sheed and Ward, 1958).
17. *Ibid.*, pp. 109ff.
18. This function of the organizations has been studied by Eric Josephson, "Political Youth Organizations in Europe, 1900-1950: A Comparative Study of Six Radical Parties and Their Youth Auxiliaries" (unpublished Ph.D. dissertation, Dept. of Sociology, Columbia University, 1959).

from the European youth movements in at least two ways: they are non-ideological, and they are not connected with any adult organization into which they eventually funnel their members. Therefore, despite the absence of any data in this study on the membership rates of people under 21, it is clear that whatever functions the associations do perform they cannot be said to serve the ends of political socialization or ideological indoctrination.

In itself this conclusion is of no great significance; in the absence of any widespread commitment to politically oriented associations among adults the lack of similar associations among the young does not mean much. However, the European and American experiences may be seen as special cases of a broader process.

Adolescence in our society is a transitional period between childhood and adulthood marked by the immersion of the individual in the peer group and its "youth culture." Emergence from this special world occurs with the assumption of occupational and marriage roles, and it is about this time that whatever affiliations the individual may have had with youth organizations are definitely severed. But, as our surveys show, it is not until about the time the person is in his thirties that he is likely to become affiliated with an adult association. Before this, it would seem, his interaction is with members of his family, close friends, and possibly neighbors. What are the consequences of this gap or lag in joining associations?

Our discussion of the citizenship functions of associations indicated that, while these may easily be overstated, they nonetheless make some contribution toward those ends. If the younger individuals in our samples belonged to associations in any significant numbers, we could say that one of the functions of such membership is to continue the socialization process in much the same way early career positions continue occupational socialization begun in school—but these individuals do not belong. Does this in any way affect their political behavior? Is it possible, for example, that this lag in membership results in prolonging certain alienated attitudes of adolescence toward the adult world?

It seems likely that this may be a relevant consideration for that smallish segment of the population committed or oriented to radical ideologies. There is some evidence that young people who might be disposed to adopt some variety of socialist ideology, for example, are disenchanted with the traditional versions offered to them.[19] In part,

---

19. As examples: Barbara P. Solomon, "The University: Everybody's Goldmine," *Dissent*, 7 (Spring, 1960), 137-142; and Arthur Mitzman, "The Campus Radical in 1960," *ibid.*, 142-148.

this may be due to a lack of real knowledge of these ideologies resulting from a lack of direct interaction with those who are committed to them. On the other hand, the disenchantment may be "rational": the ideologies may have truly become fossilized and inappropriate to the contemporary world. If this is true it may be a result of a lack of interaction between an older generation and a younger generation whose different life experiences could serve as a source of fresh insights, knowledge, or, at the very least, a stimulus to rethinking persistent problems.

In terms of associations themselves, the relatively late entrance of "new blood" may have some serious consequences. If individuals enter late it means that the leadership of an older generation is prolonged, because of the length of time it takes new members to establish themselves. It is possible that the decline in the importance of such associations as lodges may be related to the fact that an older, possibly less flexible, leadership has not been capable of reorienting these organizations to new goals when faced with the declining importance of older functions.

Clearly, these speculations raise more problems than they can hope to solve. But if voluntary associations are deemed to be an important part of the life of the society, then it is important to direct attention to anything connected with the problem of recruitment.

Associations and the Working Class

It is necessary to treat the working class and the functions of associations separately if only to avoid repetition of a constant refrain. Given the low rate of working class membership in associations, whatever functional consequences flow from association membership do not affect the working class.

This conclusion represents a serious situation for the class. Thus, for the middle class non-members the citizenship functions of associations are not highly significant, since the formal education of those individuals is an effective substitute. It is precisely the working class individual who can benefit the most from membership. Similarly, the immediate life experience of that person is apt to be far narrower than that of any member of the middle class, and the further restriction of experience represents a more severe dysfunction than it does for the middle class non-member. In a sense the situation is analogous to the effects of a sales tax: some groups suffer more than do others.

In this connection we should note that there is another function of associations of particular relevance for the working class individual; that is, its function for social mobility. In order to see how association membership functions toward this end we must see some of our previous conclusions from a new perspective. Thus, the knowledge and understanding which follows from membership can represent an insight into opportunities available for mobility. So, for example, the worker who is more than a nominal member of his union can come to see through active participation that the union bureaucracy offers another channel for achieving middle class status. Similarly, by being confined to a narrow life experience the working class person has less opportunity to undergo that "anticipatory socialization" facilitating social mobility. But, once again, since he is not a member, the individual of this class faces a greater probability of failure in whatever efforts are made to rise.

What we are saying here is, of course, not new; it is merely another confirmation of what has become a standard observation.[20] The worker remains the underdog in our society partly because the conditions of his existence create a pattern of life making it difficult to seize opportunities or even to comprehend them. In short, what we have here is the familiar circle played out in one particular context: The voluntary association may serve as a mechanism facilitating a rise from the working class, but that status does not encourage membership in associations.

Mobility considerations aside, in one sense the working class has the most to gain from membership. Despite a genuine rise in the material conditions of working class life, the fact remains that there is still what may be called a general insensitivity to the class in our society. In spite of the acceptance of the principle of the welfare state, 25 per cent of the population at about the time the surveys were conducted had an annual income below $3000; unemployment figures in the society rarely drop below five million; housing conditions for millions of people are inadequate, etc. To talk of the "poor" in our society in the same sense that the nineteenth-century theorists talked of the "poor" is obviously misleading; yet the poor are with us still and barely recognized by the society. It remains insensitive to the working class poor because they do not obtrude upon its consciousness; their lack of organization keeps them well hidden, and this social invisibility maintains poverty.

The Future of Associations: A Speculation about Past and Present

It was to the American spirit of independence and distrust of authority that Tocqueville first linked the American propensity for association.

---

20. Genevieve Knupfer, "Portrait of the Underdog"; Herbert H. Hyman, "The Value Systems of Different Classes: A Social Psychological Contribution to the Analysis of Stratification," both in Reinhard Bendix and S. M. Lipset, *Class, Status, and Power* (Glencoe, Ill.: The Free Press, 1953).

Given the lack of institutional forms resulting from a society springing fully formed from the brow of Liberalism, it is easy to see why nineteenth-century observers were struck by a flourishing associational life. Nor is it difficult to understand the relative lack of vigor in contemporary associational life; previous health and present lassitude are perhaps causally related. Associations are organized about specific interests and the achievement of specific goals, because the associations of the last century performed their functions well they helped produce our contemporary society.

It is a society which is a stable political democracy, and one in which the economy functions better than the theories seeking to explain why it does so. This has resulted in a level of existence, a quality of material life, which almost justifies utopian notions of progress. To say this is not to say that all that could have been achieved has been achieved; it is not a sign of insatiable utopianism to say that the society has fallen short of what could be attained. Nonetheless, the platitudinous conclusion is inevitable: the achievement is impressive. And, to repeat, in some measure the voluntary association has played its part.

But the society may also be seen as being somewhat "static." This does not refer to the pace of social change; rather it implies that there are at the moment few *salient moral problems* which, as it were, serve to quicken the life of the society. Two examples may clarify the type of thing being referred to. In the first two decades of the present century the problems of the immigrants and the urban poor represented moral issues for Americans. In the 1930s the Great Depression was a moral as well as an economic problem.

Such problems are important, because they are probably connected with the vigor and health of associations. They provide a stimulus for organization and a focus for action. If we look at the present situation, the one area in which associations present a picture reminiscent of the accounts of the last century is in precisely that area of life in which there is a salient moral problem, and in which the society's level of achievement has lagged—the sphere of civil rights.

Apart from this issue there seems to be no other of comparable salience.[21] This does not mean that no moral issues are present; on the contrary, it takes no great insight to spot them. For example: the growth

---

21. A qualification is necessary here. Such issues as disarmament, the atom bomb, foreign policy in general, *are* salient moral problems. But they do not have the same effect on associational life as do other moral issues, because they are too ambiguous. It is difficult to formulate specific course of action representing "solutions;" associational action is stimulated most when there can be a sense that such action can be a force in influencing events. For example, what concretely is a "sane" nuclear policy in the

of leisure time contains a moral problem; the growing proportion of the aged in the society contains the seeds of moral issues; the growth of mass communications poses problems of this kind; etc. But to locate these problems is not to say they are salient enough to mobilize sentiments and behavior.

If the assumption that the vigor of associational life is related to the perception of salient moral problems is true, then we can anticipate that in the *near future* voluntary associations will not be a significant factor in American life.

Once, however, moral issues emerge as salient we may expect to see a concomitant rise in the importance of associational life. To put it another way, when the present level of achievement ceases to be satisfactory, enough impetus may be generated for further movement and further change. When and if this occurs, the voluntary association as a significant factor in American society may receive a new lease on life.

---

modern world? Can any association really influence the complex processes involved in nuclear policy? Moreover, a voluntary association active in a democratic society can be an effective force if it has a counterpart in the society which must be a party to the policy representing a "solution." In general terms, then, when moral issues involve relations *among societies*, voluntary associations are faced with a different order of problems for which their previous history and traditions may not have prepared them.

APPENDIX A

The data upon which this study is based were gathered by two surveys using national samples: one undertaken in 1954 by the American Institute of Public Opinion (352-G.P.) and the other in 1955 by the National Opinion Research Center (Survey 367). The size of the AIPO survey's sample was 2,000, and the NORC survey's sample consisted of 2,379 individuals.

Neither of these two surveys was *primarily* concerned with the problem of the extent of voluntary association membership. The only thing the two surveys have in common, aside from the question about membership in associations, is that both were designed to secure information relevant to problems of health and sickness. (From the point of view of the present research this similarity is purely fortuitous, i.e., the surveys were selected for secondary analysis for reasons of expediency.) While extent of membership was not the primary problem of either survey, the AIPO survey was undertaken as part of a larger research on participants in a particular kind of voluntary association, and this fact has some bearing on the discrepancy between the over-all figures on membership in voluntary associations which occurs between the two surveys.

The AIPO questionnaire consisted of thirty-three questions, and "What organizations or clubs, like church organizations, service clubs, fraternal clubs, do you belong to?" was question number twenty-seven. Preceding this question were nine others which explicitly directed the respondent's attention to organizations. For example: One question involved handing the respondent a card with a list of nine organizations and asking about any contributions he may have made to them. Another asked the respondent where he thought he might secure financial help if someone in his family had polio; if the respondent did not mention a specific organization he was asked if he knew of any organizations which might help him. The question immediately preceding the one about association membership was, "Have you, yourself, ever taken part in voluntary public service work to help organizations like the Red Cross, the 'March of Dimes,' the Boy Scouts, and things like that?" An affirmative answer was followed by, "What organization(s) and what did you do?"

In contrast, the NORC schedule contained 136 questions, and the next to the last one was, "Do you happen to belong to any groups or organizations in the community here?" For those responding affirmatively there were two supplementary probe questions about types of organizations and activity within them. None of the other questions referred directly or indirectly to voluntary associations.

All survey research has to contend with the problems of recall and its reliability and validity. It is axiomatic that as more cues or stimuli are provided the easier it is to remember more fully. For our purposes the central question in both surveys was the one about membership in associations, and in assessing the reliability of the answers we must take into account the entire interview. That is, one reason why over half of the AIPO survey's respondents reported voluntary association membership is that many of the questions preceding the crucial one had the latent function of stimulating the respondent's memory of his organizational affiliations. Similar cues were not provided by the questionnaire used in the NORC survey.

However, this does not mean that the AIPO figures are more valid. Here we must consider whether the survey did not at the same time motivate the respondent to conscious or unconscious distortion in his reply to the critical question. It was pointed out above that preceding the question about membership was one concerning the respondent's participation in "voluntary public service work." The behavior inquired about is a type of activity which, formally at least, is highly valued in our society, and is the basis for individual claims of prestige and esteem. The individual who truthfully answered "no" was in a socially threatening situation; the one who responded with an untruthful "yes"—a strong temptation given the situation—was likely to be in difficulties with his superego. But the next question—"Do you belong . . .?—is an opportunity for both to recoup their social and psychic fortunes. To report that one has not helped the Red Cross, etc., but is a member of other voluntary associations permits one to save face with the interviewer and negotiate with the superego. *But at the same time it is a situation made to order for unconscious distortion.* Even those who truthfully answered "yes" to the question about participation in public service work are not exempt from motivations to distortion presented by the question that followed: It offers one of those all too rare opportunities for socially approved immodesty, e.g., "Not only do I help the Red Cross but look at what else I do as a responsible, public spirited citizen." Finally, we should not overlook the fact that no doubt many individuals did not have to rely upon their unconscious to save the situation for them.

If the AIPO figure of 55 per cent, then, must be treated with some reserve, this does not imply that the other survey's figure of 36 per cent must be unreservedly accepted. The schedule used by the NORC survey was a long and complex one, and as we have pointed out the critical question came almost at the very end. It is reasonable to assume that by the time the question was asked interviewer and respondent were fatigued, and that the latter tended to hurry the interview to a close with a simple negative subtly facilitated by similar desires on the interviewer's part. In short, just as the figure of 55 per cent may be too high, the figure of 36 per cent may err in the opposite direction.

APPENDIX B

The following list of organizations is reproduced from the code sheets of the NORC survey used in this study. The category, "organizations pertaining to health," in this list *was combined with the category "civic and service" in constructing the tables of Chapter V.* This is *not* an exhaustive list of all organizations mentioned by respondents; they are *examples* of the types of organizations included in each category.

Veterans, Military, Patriotic (and auxiliaries of same)

American Legion
VFW
Disabled American Veterans
Jewish War Veterans
Catholic War Veterans

D.A.R.
Native Sons of the Golden
 West
AMVETS
Gold Star Mothers

Organizations Relating to Health (except sick benefit associations)

Hospital Board
Ladies Aid (specifically connected
 with hospital)
Nurse's Aide Club
Retail Druggists' Association
Registered Nurses Foundation

Sister Kenny Foundation
Red Cross
American Cancer Society
March of Dimes
County Medical Society
Handicap Club

Civic or Service (other than health)

Lions
Kiwanis
Rotary
Salvation Army Mission
Community Center
PTA
High School Youth Center
Boy Scouts
Camp Fire Girls
School Board Member

Women's Club
YMCA
4-H Club
Community Chest
Chamber of Commerce
National Safety Council
Junior League
Ladies' Aid (not specifically con-
 nected with hospital)

Political or Pressure Groups

League of Women Voters
WCTU
Planned Parenthood
Young Democrats

Seventh Ward Republicans
Zionists
Independent Socialist League
Americans for Democratic Action

131

Lodges, Fraternal, Secret Societies, Mutual (Sick) Benefit Associations (and auxiliaries)

Masons
Knights of Columbus
B'nai Brith
Eagles
Knights of Pythias
Elks
Moose
Rebehah
Woodmen

Sons of Italy
Shrine
PEO
Philipine Lodge
Druids
Old Timers
Hadassah
DeMolay

Church, Religious

Holy Name Society
Altar Society
Men's Club at Church
Ladies of Charity

Women's Home and Foreign Mission
Luther League
Third Order of St. Francis
American Bible Society

Economic, Occupational, Professional (other than health or labor unions)

Truck Drivers' Association
Law Enforcement Officers'
    Association
American Bar Association
Retail Grocers' Association

Merchants and Manufacturers'
    Club
Civil Engineering Association
Producers' Coop
Farm Bureau

Cultural, Educational, College Alumni (other than health)

Association for Family Living
Literary Club
Symphony Orchestra Association
Museum Board

Lecture Club
Wayne Alumnae
Farm Demonstration Unit

Social, Sports, Hobby, Recreational (except specifically church connected)

Country Club
Bridge Club
Camera Club
Swimming Club
Newcomers' Club
Singing Club
Engineers' Wives

Flower Club
Town and Country
Travel Club
American Automobile Association
Motor Club
Boating League
Homemakers' Club

BIBLIOGRAPHY

ALLARDT, ERIK, JARTTE, P., and JRYIKILA, F. "On the Cumulative Nature of Leisure Activities," *Acta Sociologica*, 3 *(1958)*, 165-72.

ALLARDT, ERIK, and PESONEN, P. "Finland," *International Social Science Journal*, 12 *(1960)*, 27-39.

ANDERSON, ROBERT T., and ANDERSON, GALLATIN. "Voluntary Associations and Urbanization," *American Journal of Sociology*, 65 *(1959)*, 265-73.

ANDERSON, W. A. "The Family and Individual Social Participation," *American Sociological Review*, 8 *(1943)*, 420-24.

AXELROD, MORRIS. "Urban Structure and Social Participation," *American Sociological Review*, 21 *(1956)*, 13-19.

————. *A Study of Formal and Informal Group Participation in a Large Urban Community:* Unpublished Ph.D. dissertation, University of Michigan, 1954.

BANFIELD, EDWARD. *The Moral Basis of a Backward Society.* Glencoe, Ill.: The Free Press, 1958.

BARBER, BERNARD. " 'Mass Apathy' and Voluntary Social Participation in the United States." Unpublished Ph.D. dissertation, Harvard University, 1945.

————. "Participation and Mass Apathy in Associations," in A. W. Gouldner, *Studies in Leadership.* New York: Harper & Bros., 1950, 477-504.

BELL, WENDELL. "Economic, Family, and Ethnic Status: An Empirical Test," *American Sociological Review*, 20 *(1955)*, 45-52.

BELL, WENDELL, and BOAT, MARION D. "Urban Neighborhoods and Informal Social Relations," *American Journal of Sociology*, 62 *(1957)*, 391-98.

BELL, WENDELL, and FORCE, MARYANNE. "Urban Neighborhood Types and Participation in Formal Associations," *American Sociological Review*, 21 *(1956a)*, 25-34.

————. "Social Structure and Participation in Different Types of Formal Associations," *Social Forces*, 34 *(1956b)*, 345-50.

BOTTOMORE, THOMAS. "Social Stratification in Voluntary Organizations," in David Glass, *Social Mobility in Britain.* Glencoe, Ill.: The Free Press, 1954.

BROWN, EMORY J. "The Self as Related to Formal Participation in Three Pennsylvania Communities," *Rural Sociology*, 18 *(1953)*, 313-20.

BUSHEE, FREDERIK A. "Social Organization in a Small City," *American Journal of Sociology*, 51 *(1945)*, 217-26.

CURTIS, RICHARD F. "Occupational Mobility and Membership in Voluntary Associations: A Research Note," *American Sociological Review*, 24 *(1959)*, 846-48.

DOTSON, FLOYD. "Patterns of Voluntary Association Among Urban Working Class Families," *American Sociological Review*, 16 *(1951)*, 687-93.

————. "A Note on Participation in Voluntary Associations in a Mexican City," *American Sociological Review*, 18 *(1953)*, 380-86.

DYNES, RUSSELL R. "The Consequences of Sectarianism for Social Participation," *Social Forces*, 35 *(1957)*, 331-34.

EVAN, WILLIAM M. "Dimensions of Participation in Voluntary Associations," *Social Forces*, 36 *(1957)*, 148-53.

FICHTER, JOSEPH H. *Social Relations in the Urban Parish.* Chicago: University of Chicago Press, 1954.

FOSKETT, JOHN M. "Social Structure and Social Participation," *American Sociological Review*, 20 *(1955)*, 431-38.

FREEMAN, H., NOVAK, E., and REEDER, L. "Correlates of Membership in Voluntary Associations," *American Sociological Review*, 22 *(1957)*, 528-33.

FREEMAN, HOWARD, and SHOWEL, MORRIS. "Differential Political Influence of Voluntary Associations," *Public Opinion Quarterly*, 15 *(1951-1952)*, 703-14.

GALLAGHER, O. R. "Voluntary Associations in France," *Social Forces*, 36 *(1957)*, 153-59.

GIST, NOEL P. "Secret Societies: A Cultural Study of Fraternalism in the United States," *The University of Missouri Studies*, 15 *(October, 1940)*, 1-184.

GOLDHAMER, HERBERT. "Participation in Voluntary Associations." Unpublished Ph.D. dissertation, University of Chicago, 1942.

GORDON, WAYNE C., and BABCHUCK, NICHOLAS. "A Typology of Voluntary Associations," *American Sociological Review*, 24 *(1959)*, 22-29.

GREER, SCOTT. "Urbanism Reconsidered: A Comparative Study of Local Areas in a Metropolis," *American Sociological Review*, 21 *(1956)*, 19-25.

———. "Individual Participation in Mass Society," in Roland Young (ed.), *Approaches to the Study of Politics.* Evanston: Northwestern University Press, 1958, 329-42.

GROSS, NEAL. "The Differential Characteristics of Acceptors and Non-Acceptors of an Approved Technological Process," *Rural Sociology*, 14 *(1949)*, 148-56.

HASTINGS, PHILIP K. "The Voter and the Non-Voter," *American Journal of Sociology*, 62 *(1956)*, 302-07.

HAY, DONALD G. "The Social Participation of Households in Selected Rural Communities in the Northeast," *Rural Sociology*, 15 *(1950)*, 141-48.

HECKSCHER, GUNNAR. "Pluralist Democracy: The Swedish Experience," *Social Research*, 15 *(1948)*, 417-61.

HERO, ALFRED O. *Voluntary Organizations in World Affairs Communication.* Boston: World Peace Foundation, 1960.

HYMAN, HERBERT. "The Values System of Different Classes: A Social Psychological Contribution to the Analysis of Stratification," in Reinhard Bendix, and S. M. Lipset (eds.), *Class, Status, and Power.* Glencoe, Ill.: The Free Press, 1953, 426-42.

———. *Survey Design and Analysis.* Glencoe, Ill.: The Free Press, 1955.

JANOWITZ, MORRIS. *The Professional Soldier.* Glencoe, Ill.: The Free Press, 1960.

JOSEPHSON, ERIC. "Political Youth Organizations in Europe, 1900-1950: A Comparative Study of Six Radical Parties and Their Youth Auxiliaries." Unpublished Ph.D. dissertation, Columbia University, 1959.

KNUPFER, GENEVIEVE. "Portrait of the Underdog," in Reinhard Bendix, and S. M. Lipset (eds.), *Class, Status, and Power.* Glencoe, Ill.: The Free Press, 1953, 255-63.

KOMAROVSKY, MIRRA. "The Voluntary Associations of Urban Dwellers," in Logan Wilson and William L. Kolb (eds.), *Sociological Analysis*. New York: Harcourt, Brace & Co., 1949, 378-91.

KORNHAUSER, WILLIAM. *The Politics of Mass Society*. Glencoe, Ill.: The Free Press, 1959.

LANE, ROBERT E. *Political Life: Why People Get Involved in Politics*. Glencoe, Ill.: The Free Press, 1959.

LAZERSFELD, P. F., BERELSON, B., and GAUDET, H. *The People's Choice*, New York: Duell, Sloan and Pearce, 1944.

LINZ, JUAN. "The Social Bases of German Politics." Unpublished Ph.D. dissertation, Columbia University, 1958.

LIPSET, SEYMOUR M. *Political Man*. Garden City: Doubleday & Co., 1960.

LIPSET, SEYMOUR, M., and BENDIX, R. *Occupational Mobility in Industrial Society*, Berkeley and Los Angeles: University of California Press, 1959.

LITTLE, KENNETH. "The Role of Voluntary Associations in West Africa Urbanization," *American Anthropologist*, 59 *(1957)*, 579-96.

LYND, ROBERT S., and LYND, HELEN M. *Middletown*. New York: Harcourt, Brace & Co., 1929.

————. *Middletown in Transition*. New York: Harcourt, Brace & Co., 1937.

MACCOBY, HERBERT. "The Differential Political Activity of Participants in Voluntary Associations," *American Sociological Review*, 23 *(1958)*, 523-32.

MARTIN, WALTER T. "A Consideration of Differences in the Extent and Location of Formal Associational Activities of Rural-Urban Fringe Residents," *American Sociological Review*, 17 *(1952)*, 687-94.

MATHER, WILLIAM G. "Income and Social Participation," *American Sociological Review*, 6 *(1941)*, 680-83.

MAYNTZ, RENATE. "Leisure, Social Participation, and Political Activity." Bureau of Applied Social Research, Columbia University, 1960. (Dittoed.)

MAYO, SELZ C. "Age Profiles of Social Participation in Rural Areas of Wake County, S. C.," *Rural Sociology*, 15 *(1950)*, 242-51.

MAYO, SELZ C., and MARSH, C. PAUL. "Social Participation in the Rural Community," *American Journal of Sociology*, 57 *(1951)*, 243-47.

MILLS, C. WRIGHT. "The Middle Classes in Middle Sized Cities," in Logan Wilson and William L. Kolb (eds.), *Sociological Analysis*. New York: Harcourt, Brace & Co., 1949, 443-53.

MILNE, R. S. "New Zealand," *International Social Science Journal*, 12 *(1960)*, 63-68.

MITZMAN, A. "The Campus Radical in 1960," *Dissent*, 7 *(Spring, 1960)*, 142-148.

O'DEA, THOMAS F. *American Catholic Dilemma: An Inquiry into the Intellectual Life*. New York: Sheed and Ward, 1958.

PARRY, HUGH J., and CROSSLEY, HELEN M. "Validity of Responses to Survey Questions," *Public Opinion Quarterly*, 14 *(Spring, 1950)*, 61-80.

REIGROTZKI, ERICH. *Sociale Verflechtungen in der Bundersrepublik*. Tubingen: Mohr-Subeck, 1956.

RIESMAN, DAVID. *Faces in the Crowd*. New Haven: Yale University Press, 1952.

REISSMAN, LEONARD. "Class, Leisure, and Social Participation," *American Sociological Review*, 19 *(1954)*, 76-84.

ROKKAN, S. "Electoral Activity, Party Membership and Organizational Influence," *Acta Sociologica,* 4 *(1959),* 25-37.

ROSE, ARNOLD M. *Theory and Method in the Social Sciences.* Minneapolis: University of Minnesota Press, 1954.

———. "Attitudinal Correlates of Social Participation," *Social Forces,* 37 *(1959),* 202-06.

ROSSI, PETER. *Why People Move.* Glencoe, Ill.: The Fress Press, 1955.

SCAFF, ALVIN H. "The Effect of Commuting on Participation in Voluntary Associations," *American Sociological Review,* 17 *(1952),* 215-20.

SCOTT, JOHN. "Membership and Participation in Voluntary Associations," *American Sociological Review,* 22 *(1957),* 315-26.

SILLS, DAVID. *The Volunteers.* Glencoe, Ill.: The Fress Press, 1957.

SLATER, CAROL. "Class Differences in Definition of Role and Membership in Voluntary Associations in Urban Married Women," *American Journal of Sociology,* 65 *(1960),* 616-19.

SOLOMON, B. P. "The University: Everybody's Goldmine," *Dissent,* 7 *(Spring, 1961),* 137-142.

SPINARD, W. "Trade Union Participation," *American Sociological Review,* 25 *(April, 1960),* 237-244.

SROLE, L. "Social Integration and Certain Corollaries," *American Sociological Review,* 21 *(December, 1956),* 709-716.

DE TOCQUEVILLE, ALEXIS. *Democracy in America.* 2 vols. New York: Vintage Books, 1954.

VIDICH, ARTHUR J., and BENSMAN, JOSEPH. *Small Town in Mass Society.* Princeton: Princeton University Press, 1958.

WARNER, W. LLOYD, and LUNT, PAUL S. *The Social Life of a Modern Community.* New Haven: Yale University Press, 1941.

WEBBER, IRVING L. "The Organized Social Life of the Retired in Two Florida Communities," *American Journal of Sociology,* 59 *(1954),* 340-46.

WILLEMS, EMILIO. "Protestantism as a Factor of Culture Change in Brazil," *Economic Development and Cultural Change,* 3 *(1955),* 321-33.

WRIGHT, CHARLES R., and HYMAN, HERBERT. "Voluntary Association Memberships of American Adults: Evidence from National Sample Surveys," *American Sociological Review,* 23 *(June, 1958),* 284-94.

ZETTERBERG, HANS L. "National Pastime: Pursuit of Power," *Industria International 1960-61,* Stockholm, 1960, pp. 105-107, 156-168.

ZIMMER, BASIL G. "Farm Background and Urban Participation," *American Journal of Sociology,* 61 *(1956),* 470-75.

ZIMMER, BASIL G., and HAWLEY, AMOS, H. "Suburbanization and Church Participation," *Social Forces,* 37 *(1959a),* 348-54.

———. "The Significance of Membership in Voluntary Associations," *American Journal of Sociology,* 65 *(1959b),* 196-201.

INDEX

A

Age
  and membership, 30f, 33f, 38f, 117
  ideology, 117f
  mobility, 71
  status in the community, 47, 71
  sex and membership, 31, 39f
  types of associations, 71ff, 81, 83
  See also: Depression; Education; Income; Integration, Social; Ownership-Rental of Residence; Size of Community

Allardt, E., 20, 97

Anomie, 93f

Axelrod, M., 19, 34, 115

B

Banfield, E., 20

Barber, B., 109

Bell, W., 34

Bendix, R., 47

Bensman, J., 77

Brown, E., 19

C

Community Orientation, 69, 73

Consequences of Membership, 87ff
  Anomie, 93f
  "awareness" and "insight", 95
  knowledge of community organizations, 94ff, 103
  knowledge of March of Dimes sponsor, 94ff, 103
  participation in voluntary public service work, 96f, 105
  perception of community health problems, 95f, 104

Consequences of Membership—*Contd.*
  perception of future income, 92ff, 104
  perception of serious community problem, 95f, 104
  predictability of the future, 91ff, 101
  reading of books, 87ff, 98, 100
  reading of magazines, 87ff, 98, 100
  See also: Functions of Associations

Crossley, H., 14

D

Depression
  and membership, 31
  and moral problems, 120

Dotson, F., 20, 34

E

Education
  and membership, 14f, 21f
  age and membership, 31f, 41f
  "cosmopolitan-local" orientation, 79
  knowledge of community organizations, 94, 103
  knowledge of March of Dimes sponsor, 94, 103
  participation in voluntary public service work, 96f, 105
  perception of community health problems, 95f, 104
  perception of serious community problem, 95f, 104
  political party identification and membership, 48f, 58
  predictability of the future, 91ff, 101
  reading of books, 87ff, 99
  reading of magazines, 87ff, 99
  religion and membership, 51, 62f
  sex and membership, 30, 36f

DATE DUE

SEP 20 '68			
OCT 2 6 1984 ARREL			
MY 23'67			
GAYLORD			PRINTED IN U.S.A.